Mental Toughness

The Extreme Guide to Build an Unbeatable, Strong and Resilience Mind, With the Leadership's Mindset.
The Training for Success Like a Navy Seals.

Jocko Babin & Ray Manson

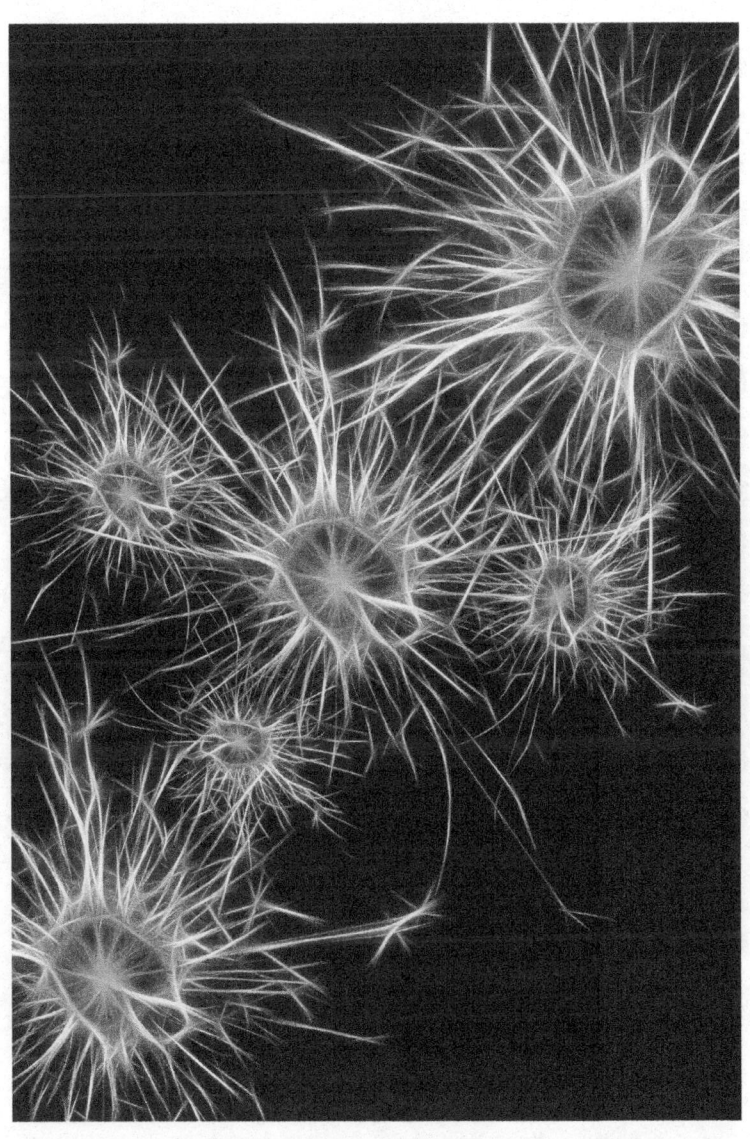

Table of Contents

MENTAL TOUGHNESS	1
TABLE OF CONTENTS	4
INTRODUCTION	8
CHAPTER 1: WHAT IS MENTAL TOUGHNESS?	10
CHAPTER 2: TRAITS OF THE UNBEATABLE MIND	23
CHAPTER 3: WHY DEVELOP MENTAL STRENGTH?	54
CHAPTER 4: HOW TO BUILD MENTAL STRENGTH	69
CHAPTER 5: FEAR AND STRESS	87
CHAPTER 6: SETTING GOALS	109
CHAPTER 7: EMOTIONAL INTELLIGENCE	120
CONCLUSION	140

© Copyright 2019 by Jocko Babin & Ray Manson - All rights reserved.

The following Book is reproduced below with the goal of providing information that is as accurate and reliable as possible. Regardless, purchasing this Book can be seen as consent to the fact that both the publisher and the author of this book are in no way experts on the topics discussed within and that any recommendations or suggestions that are made herein are for entertainment purposes only. Professionals should be consulted as needed prior to undertaking any of the action endorsed herein.

This declaration is deemed fair and valid by both the American Bar Association and the Committee of Publishers Association and is legally binding throughout the United States.

Furthermore, the transmission, duplication, or reproduction of any of the following work including specific information will be considered an illegal act irrespective of if it is done electronically or in print. This extends to creating a secondary or tertiary copy of the work or a recorded copy and is only allowed with the express written consent from the Publisher. All additional right reserved.

The information in the following pages is broadly considered a truthful and accurate account of facts and as such, any inattention, use, or misuse of the information in question by the reader will render any resulting actions solely under their purview. There are no scenarios in which the publisher or the original author of this work can be in any fashion deemed liable for any hardship or damages that may befall them after undertaking information described herein.

Additionally, the information in the following pages is intended only for informational purposes and should thus be thought of as universal. As befitting its nature, it is presented without assurance regarding its prolonged validity or interim quality. Trademarks that are mentioned are done without written consent and can in no way be considered an endorsement from the trademark holder.

Introduction

Congratulations on downloading *Mental Toughness* and thank you for doing so.

The following chapters will discuss exactly what is mental toughness, how you can achieve and improve your mental toughness, the benefits of having mental toughness, traits and characteristics of a person who has mental toughness. You will also discover how fear and stress interact with mental toughness and how developing your mental toughness can help you deal with these two issues. You will also learn more about setting goals and how mental toughness can help you achieve these goals more effectively and efficiently.

Furthermore, you will learn a great deal about emotional intelligence, including what emotional intelligence is, and when and how to use it. There are many ways in which having a higher level of emotional intelligence can benefit you. You will learn how to develop and use these skills by reading this book, so that by the end it, you will have a comprehensive understanding of what emotional intelligence is and how to hone and utilize these skills to improve your life. There are plenty of books on this subject on the market, thanks again for choosing this one! Every effort was made to ensure it is full of as much useful information as possible. Please enjoy!

Chapter 1: What is Mental Toughness?

Mental toughness may mean something different to you than it means to someone else. Oftentimes, people think about surmounting hurdles and challenges that present themselves in order to keep pushing forward toward a goal. But what allows a person to form the drive and motivation to desire and believe that he can achieve that goal, and then to formulate a plan to achieve that goal? What gets the person to stop procrastinating and take steps toward achieving that goal? And what allows the person to stay focused, not get frustrated, not give up and follow through on trying to achieve that goal until he actually achieves it? Mental toughness is what it takes to channel your motivation, determination, and desire to achieve the objective you've set.

It takes mental toughness to be on your way to achieving your goals and to take all of the steps that are listed above without getting sidetracked by distractions, emotions, thoughts, and other things that can take you off of your path.

In fact, everything that a person wants to achieve in life takes some degree of mental toughness. How much mental toughness it takes is based on the difficulty of the goal. This is especially true because things may not always be easy for you to do and your goals may not be easy to accomplish. Learning how to develop your mental toughness can help you tremendously when setting out to achieve your goal. In fact, it is so important that you have a significant degree of mental toughness when trying to achieve the goals that you have in life. Education, money, and connection may all come in second, third, and fourth to having the mental toughness and fortitude to establish your goal, stick to it, and believe that you can achieve it.

Mental toughness is often thought of as resilience - the ability to withstand what life throws at you and to keep going. One example of this comes into play when discussing mental toughness and professional athletics. If a major league baseball pitcher walks three batters in a row, he still must have the resilience to stand on the mound and pitch to the next batter even though the crowd might be booing, the backup pitcher may be warming up, the coach may be yelling at him, and his teammates are disappointed.

Why Do You Need Mental Toughness?

> *Mental toughness is required to manage emotions.*
>
> *Mental toughness is required to control and handle your thoughts.*
>
> *Mental toughness is the key to willpower.*
>
> *Mental toughness is required to navigate through trying times.*
>
> *Mental toughness is required for everyday life situations.*

Why Do You Need Mental Toughness?

Your mental state is just as important, if not more important, than the amount of knowledge, skill or money you have when you are trying to achieve a goal. There are a lot of people out there with the knowledge and education that they need to accomplish big dreams, but they do not have the proper mental state to do so. They may state moving along the way toward a goal and then back down for fear that they may fail, it will take too long, be too difficult, or somehow has otherwise become impossible. In fact, many people fail to state on their way toward achieving big goals at all because either they do not believe that it can be done, or they do not have the strength of mind to think that they can do it.

Mental toughness can provide you the inner strength that you need to be on your way to achieving your goals. Much of a person's inner strength to persevere and achieve is derived from his or her mental state. Thus, it is important for you to have a strong, stable mental state in which you can think clearly and, understand your emotions and desires, and take active steps toward achieving your goals.

Mental toughness is required to manage emotions.
It is unavoidable that people will experience emotions. Emotions are a naturally occurring state of mind that is the result of a person's surrounds, mood, and relationships and interactions with other people. Because emotions are naturally occurring, they may actually overtake a person's thoughts and become their main focus if a person lets them do so. This is where mental toughness comes in. Mental toughness gives a person the ability to control, to some extent, his or her emotions, as well as the way in which he or she reacts to them and how much these emotions take over the person's mind.

For instance, you may have had a fight with your spouse or significant other in the morning which has you stressed out, sad or feeling some other emotion that is not conducive to getting a great deal of work done. Some people may not get much accomplished that day or even irritate their co-workers or make mistakes on the job because they are focusing on their emotions. A person who has mastered mental toughness, however, should be able to perform at a high level even if he or she still cares about the argument and has experienced some of the same emotions as the person who messes up at work that day. The saying 'it's not what happens to you, it's how you handle it' is true to a significant extent.

Thus, mental toughness is very important when you seek to handle your emotions properly so that you can make wise and effective decisions while still experiencing emotions.

Mental toughness is required to control and handle your thoughts.

Thoughts differ from emotions due to the fact that they are not always about feelings. In fact, a significant portion of our time is spent thinking about things that do not have much to do with our emotions. You may think about whether or not you are going to be able to finish your homework or work project on time. Although the thought of not finishing the assignment on time may evoke some feelings and emotions, the thought of whether or not you will finish the assignment on time is not primarily based on emotion.

In order to think clearly and focus, you need to be able to control your thought. However, a challenge arises when there is a lot of things that are going on around you, and you find it difficult to focus on or even identify what is and what is not important. This is why it is so important to have mental toughness. Mental toughness can help you to control your thought processes so that you can focus and concentrate on the things that you need to be focused on or the task at hand despite whatever is going on in the world around you.

There are some key people who are known to need and have an exceptional level of mental toughness. People such as performer and world-class athletes must possess a tremendous amount of mental toughness to perform in front of millions of people and excel without getting distracted by the crowd noise, problems at home, worries that they have and more. Examples of people who possess this type of mental toughness include people such as Beyoncé, NFL players, Tiger Woods, and more. Beyoncé must get up on stage and perform for crowds of thousands of people on the day of the concert whether she is feeling happy, sad, sick or tired. She must remain focused to hit her dance steps perfectly, remember her songs even with the crowd noise and some of the fans singing along.

Furthermore, the amount of talent that she has would not get her to where she is alone. She had to have the drive to get to the top, and she had to be determined along the way and stay focused. There are a lot of other singing acts and groups that were around when she started that were considered to be just as good as Destiny's Child from which she came. Many of these groups and the singers in them are no longer around because they did not have the mental toughness to forge along through all of the struggles and hurdles that it takes to get to the top of the music field.

In fact, many people may not even want to be where Beyoncé is because they understand that it is too much mental pressure for them to handle. Many people would like to accomplish much smaller goals with far fewer people watching in order to minimize the mental pressure that is put upon them. This is why most of the articles and books that you find about mental toughness are focused on professional athletes and major performers, so much so that they often neglect giving advice to the average layman about how he can utilize mental toughness in his daily life. Throughout this book, however, you will learn how to develop mental toughness even if you never plan to play a professional sport or get up on a stage and perform for a crowd of millions because everyone can benefit from developing and increasing their mental toughness to that they can move to new heights in their own lives.

Just think about how much mental toughness a major league baseball player must have to stand at the plate with a baseball being thrown in his direction so close to him at almost 100 miles an hour if not more. He must be able to block out the crowd and not let the number of people who are watching cloud his judgment in any way. This is not an easy feat to accomplish, but it is a necessary one is he is to have any chance of succeeding at the game.

Mental toughness is the key to willpower.
Most people would be surprised to find out that willpower or lack thereof is the primary obstacle that most people face when trying to better themselves. You would probably assume that it would be money, race or class; however, in this day and age, it is possible to achieve almost anything that you want in spite of these obstacles which used to limit people in the past but are no longer considered to be hurdles today. The lack of the ability to stick to something and see it through and have the determination to make it to a set target is the obstacle that people face. This is something that is within your control; therefore, a lot of people think that they can make a few small adjustments and they will have the willpower and the determination that they need to accomplish something that they want to do. They soon find out that they were wrong when they thought that gaining willpower meant a few small changes and they were on their way toward the end goal that they desired. No, willpower takes *a lot* of major changes and hard work. The main thing that you need to change to gain more willpower is your mind. Mental toughness plays a substantial role in willpower as willpower is considered to be one of the key traits that those who have mental toughness display.

Mental toughness is required to navigate through trying times.

During times when you are doing well, have some money in the bank, your relationships are good, you are in good health, and you are rather happy, mental toughness may not be called in as much unless it is I certain high-pressure situations. However; if you ever experience hard times such as the death of a spouse or a child, loss of a job and source of income, a natural disaster or something of that nature, it is very important for you to have mental toughness to get through the situation that you are in the best that you can and get back on your feet. Hard times really are a test of your will. And hard times can happen to anybody whether they expect it and have planned for it or not.

To be prepared for whatever life throws at you and prepared for a hard time should you experience them, it is good to develop some mental toughness skills in advance. In fact, if you have never experienced true hard times, things that would not seem like as big a deal to someone who has may seem like a bigger deal to you. Thus, you will feel that you need some mental toughness to navigate through life and succeed.

Mental toughness is required for everyday life situations.

Suppose you are driving your care, the same car that you had for the last four years, down a road and you swerve to avoid hitting a deer than just ran into the street and run off of the road. As your car is careening toward a group of trees whether you go into full panic mode and let fate take over or you attempt to steer depends on how much mental toughness you have. I experienced a similar situation, and the main thing that I found out is that a group of trees looks much denser from the road; however, the trees are far enough apart that you can steer through them if you have the wherewithal to do so. A friend of mine was a passenger in a car in which a car accident was about to occur. Instead of trying to help the driver concentrate on steering, she suggested that we all pray together (The driver ignored her suggesting and used navigation skills instead of prayer to avoid the accident). If my friend in the driver's seat had been the driver when my car ran off the road, I do not believe that she would have made it because she may have been to in shock to realize that steering and maneuvering through the trees somewhat is possible.

One of the reasons that my friend may not have survived if she had been in the first car accident is that she does not possess the same amount of mental toughness that I have conditioned myself to utilize, especially in tough and trying situations. I would say she lacks a substantial amount of mental toughness; however, some people may disagree and argue that she possesses a normal amount of mental toughness. This is a skill she may never have tried to hone. But then you can look at the fact that she wanted to go to graduate school, but she didn't because she didn't believe that's he could get the money or would have the time. I, on the other hand, graduated from graduate school because I did not look for the hurdles to stop me, I looked for the hurdles to go.

In everyday life, situations that require mental toughness often present themselves and for you to get through the situation intact, you need to have already developed some mental toughness skills that will allow you to handle that specific situation. Therefore, it is wise for you to take some of the practice lessons in this book to heart and learn some skills for enhancing your mental toughness so that you can handle life at your best.

Chapter 2: Traits of the Unbeatable Mind

The unbeatable mind is strong and tough. It is resilient and relentless. It is determined, and it has the willpower and the drive to succeed. We all want an unbeatable mind and often get frustrated when we fall short of what we wanted to accomplish because we just could not stay focused and determined. Focus and determination are both products of having mental strength. These are some of the traits that the unbeatable mind people possess.

There are certain traits or characteristics that a person must possess in order to develop and establish mental toughness. Some of these traits are some important that if you do not possess them, you may need to take the time to develop these traits before you can hope to gain mental toughness.

Traits of the Unbeatable Mind

1) Mental Competency
2) Emotional Intelligence
3) Resilience
4) Willpower
5) A Winner's Mind
6) The Ability to Focus
7) They Surround Themselves with Other People Who Are Mentally Tough
8) They Avoid Trying Too Hard to Go Against the Grain
9) Expect Delayed Gratification
10) Consistency, Consistency, Consistency

Trait 1: Mental Competency

The first trait that you must possess to develop and sustain a certain level of mental toughness is mental competency. Having a sound and competent mind is the very first thing that you need to gain mental toughness. Mental competency is the ability to make sound judgement decisions. Thus, it is important to pay attention to and take care of your mental health before developing your mental competence. Taking care of your mental health is important to having the proper foundational environment for mental toughness to develop. Disorders such as bipolar disorder can cloud your judgement and make it very difficult for you to develop mental toughness.

Don't assume that your mental health and mental competency does not change when certain things in your life change. If you experience something such as a death or a severe emotional loss or you are going through post-partum depression, or you just entered menopause, take the time to go get your mental health checked out. This is a very important step to developing an unbeatable mind.

Trait 2: Emotional Intelligence
Emotional intelligence can be characterized as a type of emotional competency, similar to mental competency for the emotions. Emotional competency is the ability to identify, understand and control your own emotions while being able to identify and understand the emotions of others and adjust properly to these emotions.

Having a low level of emotional intelligence can make it very hard to succeed in areas of life that involve other people. For instance, a person who lacks emotional intelligence may find it hard to succeed in relationships due to the fact that he cannot identify and understand the emotions of potential dates and mates. This may lead to a significant amount of communication issues, a lack of enjoyment in the relationship, and the inability to form relationships altogether.

Moreover, having a low level of self-awareness can cause you to identify your own emotions improperly. You may fail to realize how you truly feel about a person, job, or issue because you were not in touch with your emotions. This can lead to less satisfaction in these areas of your life. A high level of emotional intelligence leads to self-awareness. A person who has mastered emotional intelligence skills is more likely to do things that lead to a higher level of satisfaction for him or her because he or she knows himself better

People who excel in the area of emotional intelligence, however, may find it very easy to deal with people and gravitate toward people. The reason that these people tend to gravitate toward other people is that people have a tendency to reach to them well. There are two key factors which have a significant impact on the way in which people react to them, and these are 1) empathy and 2) and increased ability to communicate with others.

Empathy is the ability to understand the thoughts and feelings of another person. It is the ability to put yourself in their shoes so to speak. People who can empathize with others are more likely to make other people comfortable around them and feel relaxed. Furthermore, people tend to feel that the empathetic person cares more about their day or how they are doing than people who have not developed the skill to emphasize with others. This can lead to deeper connections. Thus, a person who has emotional intelligence and can emphasize with others is more like to have more positive strong connections with people than a person who does not know how to emphasize with others. And these strong connections are a support system upon which a person can build more mental toughness.

A person with emotional intelligence has better communication skills. Being able to understand other people's emotions and adjust accordingly aids in conversation skills tremendously. Understanding the emotions of others can keep you from saying things which are off-putting or offensive, both thing that can quickly end a conversation and convince the other person not to communicate as much with you in the future.

Communication skills are derived from not only having the ability to understand emotions and speech; it includes reading and understanding the use of body language, personalities and more. Much of communication is about listening. To be a good listener, you should learn to listen actively. Do not just stand there passively as a conversation is taking place, that a strong interest in the words that are being said. And be sure that you notice the facial expression and the body language. Hand gestures are also good for you to notice. Take in the whole scene and make a judgement with that in mind.

Trait 3: Resilience
Resilience is the cornerstone trait of mental toughness. In fact, many people consider resilience to be the definition of mental toughness. Resilience is the ability to persevere and persist even though the challenges that life brings you. It is the ability to dust yourself off after a setback and get back up and try again and again until you succeed. Resilience is what helps people to overcome the challenges and obstacles that they find when they start trying to achieve a certain goal.

There are a number of factors that make up resilience. One of the factors that play a role in resilience is possessing confidence in yourself. You must have confidence in order to succeed. Confidence is the belief that you can accomplish the goal that you have set out to accomplish, that you are good enough, and you deserve to achieve your goal. To achieve a lofty goal, you have to believe that you can.

Therefore, confidence is also the ability to limit and control your negative beliefs in yourself so that they do not outweigh the positive ones that are telling you that you can succeed. Throughout life, many people have formed a significant amount of negative beliefs about whether or not they can be something that they want to be or do something that they want to do. People may have been led to believe that they are limited by where they are from, how much money they have, their skin color, their looks and more. These beliefs tend to reside in the back of people's minds and stop them from believing that they can achieve certain goals in life and that they need to 'stay in their place' and dream they type of dreams that were made for someone like them. Peers, teachers, classmates and more may have discouraged a person from trying to hieve certain goals instead of encouraging the person to go after them. Therefore, resilience is the ability to get past these negative affirmations that have been placed in our minds, sometimes over the span of years, and to reprogram ourselves to see our chances of achieving these goals in a more positive manner.

Trait 4: Willpower

People who are mentally tough have a significant amount of willpower. Willpower is the determination that is needed to do things such as lose 50 pounds, stop smoking, stick to an exercise routine and many other things in life.

Willpower is the ability to not give in to your negative desires. It is the ability to resist temptation in order to make changes in your life that will improve your life from its current state. In fact, a survey conducted by the American Psychological Association, it was found that the number 1 barrier that most people cited to making positive changes in their lives was the lack of willpower. Therefore, the most limiting factor that people face, according to the American Psychological Association is not the lack of money, lack of education, or the lack of time, it is the lack of the ability to resist negative temptation.

Willpower or lack thereof is one of the biggest hurdles that most people face. In order to quit smoking, you need to be able to withstand the urge to do so; but, the majority of people who try to quit smoking fail because their desire to quit is not as strong as their desire to smoke one more cigarette. Even though smokers who want to quit may be aware of all of the negative effects that smoking can have has on them such as a wide variety of health problems, high cost, stained teeth, walls and more, people still lack the sheer determination to quit the habit. A person who has mental toughness, however, is able to channel this determination and use it to effectively quit smoking. And willpower is the key to success in most of the goals that you have in life.

Trait 5: A Winner's Mind
Mentally tough people have the right mindset to achieve the task that they set out to achieve. They believe that they can do it and have a positive attitude and the likelihood that they will succeed. Having a winner's mind is about having the drive to push

forward and not allowing yourself to take no for an answer. People with a winner's mind do have the willpower that is necessary to achieve the goals and dreams; in fact, this is something that many people with a winner's mind never even bother to call into question, unlike the rest of us.

Certain aspects are present within the winner's mind. A winner's mind is grateful for the things that he or she has. Being thankful for the things that you have allows you to have a positive attitude despite the things that you lack. A winner is glad for the everyday things that he or she was blessed with that will allow him or her to achieve his or her goals in life.

A winner's mind thinks positive thoughts. There are many people who allow their minds to be clogged with negative thoughts. This is something that is detrimental to their spirit, their mindset, and their likelihood of achieving the goals that they set out to accomplish. Winners concentrate on seeing things in a positive manner. In fact, winners try to surround themselves with a positive vibe and group of people altogether so that their mindset is connected to positivity.

In addition, a winner's mind is always ready and open to learn more and enhance the skills that the person possesses. Winners are constantly learning and developing and evolving in order to stay on top of their game.

Winners are always setting new goals. Once you reach one goal in life, a winner would not be satisfied to just sit back and be content that he or she had achieved that particular goal. Winner's tend to set new goals immediately after achieving one goal; the success of fulfilling one the first goal offers encouragement and confidence that the next goal that is set can be achieved as well. Winners also tend to set these goals in progression, or series, one right after the other, knocking them off like a to-do list. This helps to keep you motivated and striving to achieve more and more.

Trait 6: The Ability to Focus
We've all seen people who do not have a strong ability to focus and are easily distracted. In fact, there is a good chance that you are one of these people if you have not taken the time to try to develop your mental toughness. Mental strength improves your concentration. A significant number of exercises that

are designed to help you improve your mental strength are focused on concentration.

Many high-performance athletes have tunnel vision when in their athletic performance mode so that they have a total and complete concentration that allows them to excel. This focus is necessary to make split-second decisions on how to deal with other players in order to come out on top. Many people who have never participated in these types of activities do not understand the type of focused zone these athletes get into and may have never honed their skills to get to total focus on the play at hand.

Trait 7: They Surround Themselves with Other People Who Are Mentally Tough

People with mental toughness tend to surround themselves with other people who are mentally tough. You often find that athletes and entertainers of a certain level tend to associate with each other, and you may have assumed that it is because they are celebrities or because they are highly paid. You may not realize that their work ethic may be part of the reason that they gravitate towards each other. Their careers are so demanding that other people may not understand this and may not agree with doing the same amount of work that they are willing to put in. These high-level performers keep each other on their toes and encourage each other.

And these people all possess a high degree of mental toughness which tends to feed off of each other. They can encourage each other to stay strong and work hard. They illustrate what mental toughness is in a given situation; they support each other and more.

It is rare that you see a person who seems to be strong mentally and emotionally closely associated with someone who is significantly weaker in these two categories. This is because, although the stronger one may rub off on and have an effect on the weaker one, the weaker one has an effect on the stronger one as well. The stronger one is being pulled down, and the weaker one is being pulled up toward a common average strength. This is often uncomfortable for both people. It can be frustrating for the stronger person who may often wonder why the weaker one fails to show as much willpower, determination, and drive, and it can be belittling for the weaker person who may experience insults and a condescending attitude from the other. Thus, it is beneficial for both people in associate more closely with someone on their level of mental strength.

This means that if you desire to develop your mental strength, you need to identify and surround yourself with people who possess mental strength as well. And you may have to eliminate or reduce association with some people who may keep you from reaching higher levels of mental strength.

Trait 8: They Avoid Trying Too Hard to Go Against the Grain
No, you should not always try to simply go with the flow and fit in. And the people known for having very high levels of emotional intelligence definitely stand out; however, there is nothing wrong with trying to fit in a little. Constantly trying to buck the system can get tiring and start to become frustrating.

In addition, this can place more stress and mental strain on a person. This takes up space in a person's minds and takes a good deal of his or her time that could have been spent on something else. Furthermore, trying to be different can start to take a toll on you emotionally. When working on improving emotional intelligence which is covered later in this book, you will learn to identify and understand other people's feelings and reactions and how to adjust to gain better responses from others.

Trait 9: Expect Delayed Gratification
People with mental strength do not need to reap immediate benefits for their work and actions. They are fine with the benefits coming in time for the work that they did and the time that they put in. Seeking instant gratification can keep you from achieving what you could have achieved if you understood that the payout for the work that you put in does not always come immediately. Sometimes, it may take years to see the fruits of your labor. It is still important to keep going in order to see the benefits of your work.

Honing your mental strength will allow you to see that rewards are not the only good thing that you receive from your hard labor. There is the pride of a job well done and accomplishing your goals. You can also enjoy helping others in some way. And the rewards for your hard labor will come in time.

Trait 10: Consistent, Consistent, Consistent
People with mental toughness are consistent. Consistency goes along with expecting delayed

gratification and patience; however, it does differ slightly. As previously stated, one of the most notable times when we discuss mental strength is with professional athletics. It is very important for professional athletes to be able to perform consistently at a high level. When watching an NFL game, you often hear the quarterback being judged on his consistency. One great play or game is not enough; to be the starting quarterback whom the team builds their offense around and has kids wearing his jersey, he must be consistency through the plays of the game, game after game.

Consistency is not just important in sports; it is important in life in general. It is vital that a doctor in the operating room is consistent and that a trial lawyer is consistent with his results. Consistency is the ability to produce the same high- quality results over and over again. This is done by understanding what you did right and how you did it as well as what you did wrong and what you need to do to fix it. After you identify what you did right, make sure that you *study* your performance to understand exactly how you did it so that you can repeat it. If you did it differently from others and still got it right. Was it luck? Luck will not allow you to produce consistency. To be consistent, there must be a solid foundation based on knowledge skill, and practice as well as performance in real-world situations.

Try to understand where and why you differed. If your correct answer or means of doing something differed from the norm, examine where and how it differed and assess whether the normal way would be easier for *you* to perform. addition, you may want to examine which way is capable of being reproduced repeatedly.

To be consistent, one must practice, practice, practice, and learn, learn. You have to understand how things are done step by step in order to be consistent. This takes a more thorough interest in and understanding of what you are doing than having a few great performances.

Common Habits of People with Mental Toughness

Be Calm, Cool and Collected
Not Wasting Time Concentrating on Things You Cannot Control
Leave the Past in the Past but Learn from It
Change Yourself but Don't Try to Change Others
Don't Waste Time on Envy and Jealousy
Not Spending a Great Deal of Time Worrying About What Others Think About You
Be Thankful for Everything That You Have
Don't Criticize
Live in the Present, Not the Future

Common Habits of People with Mental Toughness

Be Calm, Cool and Collected

The first habit that people with mental toughness display that you should try to emulate is that of caring themselves as if they are cool, calm, collected and in control of every situation that they are in. And they do this, even if they are not completely sure that they can control the situation.

Acting and thinking as if you are leaving parts of a situation up to luck and prayer, although this may seem like it brings hope to many people, can cause you to feel that you are not in control of the situation and you are powerless to truly control what is going on around you and the situation that you are in.

Feeling and acting as if you are in control can give you an underlying mindset that you have control over the world around you. This mentality has a significant impact on the way that you think and behave.

Not Wasting Time Concentrating on Things You Cannot Control

In fact. Spending a significant amount of time and energy thinking about the things that are beyond your control or that you cannot change can be draining on your energy, frustrating, a waste of time, and a confidence killer. Similar to what they say in Alcoholics Anonymous, "You need to have the courage to accept that the things that you can change and change the things that you can and have the wisdom to know the difference." People with mental toughness tend to abide by this statement even if they have never been an alcoholic. Things that are beyond your control should also be beyond your focus.

No one is blessed with endless mental energy; therefore, one habit that people with mental toughness display is the ability to stop wasting their time thinking about the things that are out of their reach or control so that they can spend more time focusing on all of the things that they have full control over.

This differs from the aforementioned being calm, cool, and collected because you can actually be calm and cool while occupying your mind and your thoughts with activities and events that are not within your control. Stay focused on things that you do have control over.

Leave the Past in the Past but Learn from It

The past does have its place, but it is definitely in the past is what people who have mastered mental toughness definitely understand.

Yes, it is important to learn from the past so that you do not repeat the same mistakes. However, you should not be overly focused on or consumed by the past. This is true whether the past was good or bad.

It is easy to understand why you should not spend a great deal of time focused on the past if it was full of negative things. However, many people often fail to realize that it is equally harmful to spend your time focusing on the past it if was great. If you were a star running back in college but hold down a regular nine to five now, spending a great deal of time going over and trying to relive the heroic moments of your past can cause you to waste time and even miss out of the present. And it is the present that prepares you for the future.

You cannot live in or relive the past. It is over. Even if the memories and the lessons from it linger, time keeps moving on, and it is best that you keep moving with it.

Part of understanding that the past is in the past is to understand that you should not bring all of the negative thoughts and feelings and experiences from the past into the present. For instance, if you were the fat girl that did not get many dates in high school and college, however, you lost 75 pounds, you need to understand that you are no longer the fat chick and you should not let the hurts of the past limit your present and future.

One way to leave the past in the past is to understand that it does not change. Thus, there is no use in going over different scenarios of what ifs. If there is a different step or direction that you believe you should have gone in in the past, figure out how to go in that direction now. And if the door has closed on that opportunity in your life, find another door that you can open.

Change Yourself but Don't Try to Change Others

In life, we often want other people around us to change so much that we try to change them; however, this is far from a great tactic to us and often a waste of time, energy, and emotions.

If you want to see changes in your life you need to make them. Take active steps to make changes that will benefit you without expecting others to change with you. This is not to say that the people around you that you care about won't be willing to change for the better, but you to see let them make the decision that they need to change on their own.

And even if you can encourage some people to change, you can't change everybody, but you can change some of the people around you. Some people in your life are not going to be willing to change, and if they are bringing you down in any way, you need to get them out of your life. It is important to know when to cut some people out of your life who are treating you negatively or otherwise having a negative effect on your life instead of hoping and waiting for them to change.

Don't Waste Time on Envy and Jealousy
In life, we often look at others and wish we had what they have. Sometimes it seems as though life is unfair because we do not have those things. There is no usefulness in spending time thinking that things are unfair and being jealous of others. In fact, when others around you experience success, you should be happy for them and proud of them in order to be in a positive state of mind. Envy is a significant energy drainer. It is a lot more prudent to spend your time figuring out how you can better yourself than wishing you had what someone else has. If you spend your time thinking about how you can get where you want to be, you may even get what they have that you are jealous of!

Not Spending a Great Deal of Time Worrying About What Others Think About You

Spending time thinking about what others think about you is often in the same category as spending time thinking about things that you cannot control. It can be a major time waster.

Yes, you do need to care what other people think about you. You can't just ignore what other people think about you. In fact, if a significant number of people seem to be thinking the same thing, then they could be right. The world is full of other people, and it is better to have them on your side than against you and can make life significantly easier. You will learn more about this later in this book when you learn about emotional intelligence.

Be Thankful for Everything That You Have

People with mental strength garner some of it from being thankful for all that they have. This can especially to true in tough times. Instead of dwelling on the things that you do not have it is often better to focus on the things that you do. This can help you persevere and get through your obstacles and trying times.

Wallowing in self-pity, the opposite of being thankful for what you have is a habit that those who desire or possess mental toughness never display. This is an energy and emotion drainer that can keep you stuck where you are during troubled times, unable to move past them.

This is why you should count your blessings. During hard times or when you need some encouragement, you should even try making a list of the things in your life that you are thankful for. And everything on the list does not have to be something big. Look around at your surroundings and in your life and try to find some small things that you can be thankful for. Noticing all of the little things around you that you can be grateful for that you overlook on a daily basis can help you to understand how lucky and blessed you are and give you the strength and mental toughness to go on day to day and pursue your life's goals.

Don't Criticize
People who are mentally tough don't spend their time complaining about and criticizing situations around them. Instead, they look of the positive aspects of things instead of focusing on the negative.

Either find some way to change whatever it is that you see that's flawed or let it go. Complaining does nothing but causes you and the people around you to hear a bunch of negative thoughts. In fact, if you have a habit of complaining, you may develop the reputation of being a negative force of a downer to people that have to listen to it.

Live in the Present, Not the Future
The present is now. Many people are aware that it is damaging to spend a great deal of time living in the past; however, you may not be as aware that it is just as damaging to spend too much time 'in the future' as well. If there are things that you need to do to achieve your goal, a new goal that you would like to achieve, something that you would like to do, or even something as simple as making sure you do something fun that day, don't wait for a more convenient time in the future to start these things.

Not wanting to live in the future is especially important when it comes to enjoying your life. It is important to take some time out to have fun and enjoy life in order to stay mentally and emotionally balanced. Because everything in life does not always work out as planned and some goals that you set you may not end up achieving, one way to avoid becoming frustrated and lose your willpower and determination is to make sure that you do some of the fun things that you have been waiting until you have more money or until your kids go off to college to do.

Lesser scale traits of mental toughness.
There are some characteristics of mentally tough people that can be seen in some of the things that they do that may not, at first, be obvious to people who are looking on. These are smaller than the aforementioned traits and characteristics of mentally tough people, but they are still worth mentioning.

1) Mentally tough people also display the ability to forgive.

It takes a mentally strong person to forgive others for things that they have done to hurt them. Holding grudges is mentally and emotionally draining and can prevent you from partaking in some opportunities. However, it is important to examine why something happened to determine if it was a one-time thing or something that is a part of a person's character. This is because even though a mentally strong person has the capacity to forgive, you still should not let the same person burn you over and over. A mentally strong person also has the ability to recognize when someone needs to be eliminated from his or her life or at least kept at a distance. That being said, forgiveness is for the forgiver. It lets a weight off of your mind and gives you inner peace with regard to the situation that took place for which you are bestowing the forgiveness.

2) They ask for help when they need it.

A lot of people may be too proud to ask for help; however, mentally tough people are strong enough to ask people for assistance when they need it. Asking for help shows that you understand your limitations and you are willing to sacrifice a small bit of pride before you fail to do something properly.

3) People with mental strength are financially responsible.

It is important to be financially responsible so that you can save money for the future and afford the things that you need. It is also important not to overextend yourself credit wise so you can buy things such as house and cars and get school loans. Mentally tough people understand this and are willing to forgo some of the little things that they would have like to have in life now in order to save money and ensure that they have good credit. In fact, short of a tragedy, the overwhelming majority of people with mental toughness have good credit.

4) Mentally tough people manage time wisely.

Just as people with mental strength manage money wisely, they also manage time wisely. People with mental strength understand that utilizing their time wisely is important to being able to achieve all that they need to do throughout the day so that they get everything that they need to get accomplished done and turned in on time. This is a sign of maturity, something that responsible people do.

    5) People with mental strength are humble. Mental strength and humility go hand and hand. People with mental strength do not need to be arrogant about their accomplishments or toot their own horn. They feel that if they do a good enough job in work, school, or life, their work and accomplishments will speak for themselves, and they can carry themselves with humility. If you feel the need to be arrogant, ask yourself 'Where are you falling short that your work and life do not already speak volumes about where you are?' Realize. However, that humble is not the same as self-deprecating. Don't try to make yourself smaller to make others comfortable; but, be a big enough person not to brag.

    6) Mentally strong people know how to pick their battles.

In life, there will be numerous times when you and other people tend to disagree. You do not always have to speak up and show it. Instead, it is often best to pick and choose when to speak up and when to let some things good for the sake of keeping things running smoothly and preserving amicable relationships. Although you should not shy away from conflict if it is necessary for you to stand up for yourself or some other important reason, you should not shy away from it either.

    7) Mentally strong people realize that although they have control over their own lives, everything in life isn't fair and they should not expect it to be.

Yes, you should believe that you have control over your own life; however, it is unrealistic to believe that simply working hard, doing all the right things, and being a good person can get you everything. Some people are born with more, some people are given things, and some people are lucky enough to win the lottery. That's life. It does not make sense to spend time thinking about whether or not everything is fair. The answer is no but that you have to live with.

    8) People with mental toughness treat others fairly.

Treating other people fairly is a very important part of being a strong-minded person. We have all seen someone who appeared to be easy to take advantage of.

And there are a number of people out there who certainly would do so. Getting something this way seems to be easy and fast, but it should also be against your morals and values.

This only gets you somewhere in the short term. It can damage your reputation and make you seem like an untrustworthy, scandalous, unreliable person who may take advantage of others. Even if the vulnerable person was the only person who you took advantage of, it is everyone would trust you less because of it. This is one thing that is not worth doing to yourself in the long run.

Chapter 3: Why Develop Mental Strength?

The answer to why develop your mental strength is a rather easy one – because if you have not taken the time to do it yet, there is a good chance that your mental strength is not as developed as it can be and you are not able to achieve your goals at the level that you would like as a result of this fact.

You should develop your mental strength so that you can be more productive in your life. Productivity and mental strength go hand and hand. It takes mental strength to concentrate on tasks and fortitude to finish them. This is especially true with complicated tasks. Productivity is one of the key factors that determine how well you perform on your job and in any other tasks that you choose to undertake in life. If you lack productivity, it may be due to lack of concentration, being distracted by your emotions, lack of drive, energy, desire, and more. To become more productive, have more success in your career and accomplish more of the things that you want to do in your life, you should practice mental strength exercises. You may even get that raise that you have wanted for so long!

You should develop your mental strength so that you can overcome challenges and hurdles. Mental strength gives you the ability to overcome challenges and hurdles. The difference between people who keep going when they reach obstacles that they need to overcome on their way to a goal and people who do not overcome these obstacles but instead turn away and decide that the tasks are too tough is that the first group possesses mental strength. Mental strength is what is needed to see a way around the hurdles that you face in life and try to go around them so that you can achieve larger goals. Thus, lacking mental strength allows you to only achieve smaller unimpeded gaols in life that are easy to attain.

If you ever desired to get a job which requires you to have a master's degree or a PhD, you can either see the hurdles ahead of you such as lack of time or lack of money or energy or you can see the opportunity for advancement in front of you and decide that these aforementioned hurdles can be surmounted. This is not too say that these hurdles are less real or apparent to the people with the mental strength to try to go past them and enroll in the school program that they want. This hurdles are just as real and may result in struggling and difficulty for a time; however, the people with mental strength are willing to handle these struggles in order to achieve the end goal whereas the people who lack mental strength try to avoid the struggles toward the gaol and thus avoid the goal itself.

You should develop your mental strength so that you feel that you have more control over your life. In order to have control over your life, you need to have mental strength. Mental strength conditions you to believe that you have the power to control the things that are going on around you.

You should develop your mental strength to adjust to change.
The world is changing everyday. Many so-called baby boomers know that when they first entered the workforce, it was far different than it is today. The use of computers was minimal, and the internet was not as popular as it is today. Social media was nonexistent. Then a change came that hit the workplace and society in general and these older members of society saw the skills that the younger generation possessed take over even after all of their years on their job and seniority. Some of these people may have had a hard time adjusting to the changes that were taking place; however, those who wanted to be successful worked

hard to make sure that they could keep up with the changes that were taking place in society so that they could fit in with the times and still have value at work that would allow them to receive the salary that they desired and qualify for the jobs that they wanted. This is something that is normally discussed with the younger generation which is just coming in to work. Flexibility and the ability to adjust to change are keys to longevity that one must possess to keep going and stay current in this world. Mental strength allows a person to realize this and make the changes that he or she needs in spite of poride or years of doing things a certain way.

Change comes at many times in our lives. Sometimes change comes when you move to a different city for a new job. Sometimes change comes around when you leave a relationship that you have been in for a while such as what occurs with a divorce and sometimes change occurs when you enter a different stage in your life. Many people try to resist adjusting to the changes that are occurring and what things to stay the same. People with mental strength, however, are mentally tough enough to understand that changes take place in life and in order for you to be successful and live life to its fullest, you need to change with it.

To establish a winner's mind

Working on and establishing mental toughness is like setting a standard of excellence for yourself that causes you to strive for a higher level of excellence that you may have ordinarily strived for had you had you not worked to cultivate your mind. It is like setting a higher level of expectations for yourself, and you are aware of what these expectations are. Oftentimes, thinking that you can do or excel at something is half the battle and when trying to establish mental toughness, conditioning your mind for winning thoughts processes is very important. Your mindset can help you with your willpower, dedication, time management, and the other essential things that you need to do to establish your goals and to succeed at the things that you set out to do.

Mental toughness promotes longevity in your career or goals

Mental toughness is what allows you to stick around in your career or at your set goals. For instance, let's say that you want to be a dancer. You must undergo a great deal of practice and training to get started. Then you go on a number of auditions, a number of which will be rejections. You may hear criticism of your skills in a not so friendly manner, maybe even a little hurtful. If you ever want to get on Broadway, you have to go through all of this and that just to make it in the show. After that, there are rehearsals, shows, and more rehearsals and shows. If you do not have a strong mind, you are not going to make it that long under these conditions. It is very important that you use your mental strength to keep pushing on and to help you understand what you are working for.

Building mental toughness allows you to stand up for the difference between right and wrong when others won't
Most people know the difference between right and wrong, but does that mean that they are willing to stand up for it? It takes mental strength to stand up for what is right when other people won't. You may feel like you are standing by yourself which can make you nervous and a little scared but you will only be able to stand up for right versus wrong if you build up enough mental toughness to withstand the crap that gets thrown at you for not staying on the
side of the majority of the people.

Mental toughness allows you to be able to handle distractions and keep your focus.

Building mental toughness allows you to keep your focus and not be swayed by distractions when they come your way. This is very important because life is full of distractions and you will run into a large number of them if you want to achieve lofty goals. This distraction will not knock you off your game as much if you have a strong mind and the ability to focus.

There are a lot of things in life that may cause someone to lose their focus. Everything that happens in life generally involves some type of emotion and not having mental toughness can allow these emotions to take over your thoughts, cloud your judgment, cause you to dwell on issues instead of using your time wisely and be an all-around distraction. Even though you may have a number of important things to do, you will find them very difficult to get done if you cannot focus. This can even lead to dangerous situations if you become distracted while driving or doing other things that really require concentration.

Mental toughness is the answer to being distracted. Although mental toughness does not allow you to block out emotions and emotional situations, it does allow you to handle your emotions and emotional situations in the proper manner so that you can address these issues at the proper time and still be able to function during the day.

Mental toughness allows you to be able to prioritize.

The new slogan Priorities First is very important. You need to handle your priorities first and then handle the rest of the stuff later. It is not okay to neglect your priorities for something that seems more enjoyable or more important. This can cause you a great deal of problems in the future, and you will regret it. Mental toughness helps you understand your priorities and your obligations no matter how many other things you need to do.

In life, there will be a great number of things that you need to get done that may cause you to neglect your priorities. This is simply a fact a life that can not be changed, and you need to have the mental toughness to figure out what your priorities are and how to get everything else done without neglecting them.

Mental toughness helps you to identify and change irrational thoughts

Mental toughness allows a person to identify irrational thoughts so that you can address these thoughts and their origins and replace them with new beliefs that are more accurate. This is very important for people to do so that they have an accurate perception of the things going on around them. People who have not established mental toughness often stick to old belief; however, people who have developed mental toughness have the strength to examine their beliefs and admit when one of them falls short from what is rational and let it go. Establishing an accurate perception is very important because your perception is your reality. Inaccurate perceptions can skew your way of thinking so that you cannot make proper judgment decisions.

Mental toughness teaches you patience
You cannot have everything at once, and mental toughness will help you with patience in the same way that it helps with willpower. You cannot expect immediate results. Time and patience are part of the key to success in the long run. You can expect to get everything at one time; therefore, patience is a virtue that mental toughness instills in us.

Mental toughness gives you greater life satisfaction

Mental toughness helps to increase a person's life satisfaction. This is because it gives you the basic tools you need to succeed and the drive to do it. Mental strong people are able to handle life, in general, better than people who lack mental strength. They are able to control their emotions, work more efficiently, they are better listeners, and they bond better with others.

The people who are the most satisfied with their lives are the people who make wise choices and exercise some form of control over themselves. It is very important to control the need to spend money, waste time, or do harmful things that seem fun at the time. Developing mental toughness affords you the mental resources to live your life more responsibly. This is the primary reason that people who have taken the time to develop mental toughness are more satisfied with their lives.

The fact that someone has spent time honing their thoughts and brain power into a winner's brain also shows determination. This means that this person is willing to do what it takes to achieve his goal and one of which is life satisfaction. Mental toughness helps you understand that it does not make sense to complain that you are not satisfied with your life and not do anything about it. There is no point in expecting anything to change unless you take steps and do something to move toward happiness.

Mentally tough people plan out goals that are the steps that move them along the way to happiness. These people do not take no for an answer. They are strong enough to face challenges that they may encounter and determined enough to make it to the point at which they feel that they can rest assured and happy that they have done all that they could do to be satisfied with the way that their lives are going and the way that it turned out.

Mental toughness is akin to inner strength, and it makes life easier in general
Developing mental toughness does for the mind what working out does for the body. It makes your brain stronger, faster, and better than it would have been if you had not taken the time to do so. Thus, mental toughness is like a workout routine for the mind that strengthens your thought processes, your emotions, and your resolve to succeed.

Just as working out makes it easier for you to walk around, jog, run, walk upstairs and participate in daily activities, working out your mind by developing your mental strength makes it easier to think under pressure, establish and fulfill goal, focus on the things that are important at the time, establish willpower and more.

Many people do not have the mental strength to make tough choices and take the steps that they need to to get them done. This makes their lives more difficult, so it is very easy to see why mental toughness makes life easier. It is much better to be mentally tough, with inner strength, than to not develop your mind just like it is much better to be physically strong than it is not to develop your body because you never know when you are going to need to use your mental strength and fitness just like you never know when you are going to need to use your physical strength and fitness. But it definitely makes life easier to have it so that you never get caught off guard. It is of utmost importance to make sure that you mental toughness skills are at their peak when you need them so that you can navigate through the things that may trip others up in life and give them a difficult time.

Mental toughness allows you to reduce stress and anxiety

Stress and anxiety, a subject that will be discussed in more detail later in this book, are harmful to your mind and body if left unchecked and allowed to fester. Stress causes a number of health problems, both mental and physical. It can affect everything in your life as well. You may become agitated when you get stressed out and take it out on those around you including family members, children, co-workers, friends, strangers and more. This can cause problems in relationships that may be hard to fix if done repeatedly, over a period of time, or the stressful situation is not fixed.

Stress is not something that should not be addressed; however, people who do not have fully developed mental toughness skills may not know how to cope with stress healthily. They may come up with negative solutions to dealing with stress such as drinking, smoking, and more. When you develop your mental toughness, however, you develop skills to help you adequately cope with stress and stressful situations so that they do not get out of control and you can handle such incidents and occurrences better.

Furthermore, people who do not have mental toughness skills suffer from more stress than people who do. There are a number of reasons that stressful situations arise. One common reason that a stressful situation occurs due to poor time management. For example, let's say that you have a project that is due on the first of the month and you have had two weeks to complete it. You know that you should start on the project immediately, yet you choose to procrastinate until you only have four days left before the project is due. If you had managed your time properly, you would have had it completed with ease; however, because you failed to manage time properly, you are down to crunch time. This can cause you to stress out about whether you will get your project done in time. In addition, you may become stressed when thinking about whether you will be able to complete the rest of your obligations. If you had developed your mental toughness skills before this situation arose, you would have been less likely to fall victim to stress. This is because you would have understood the importance of managing your time properly and had the discipline to do so.

There are many other examples of how mental toughness skills and development can help you to reduce, avoid, or alleviate stressful situations. This is because mental toughness involves discipline and being disciplined in areas of your life helps to keep you from finding yourself in negative situations which can cater to the creation of stress and anxiety.

Chapter 4: How to Build Mental Strength

Mental strength is not something that you have to be born with. It develops over time due to your life experiences, observations, associations with other people, and other factors that shape who you are. It can develop naturally over time. You do, however, have the ability to control the development of mental strength that you have. You can take steps to actively hone your mental strength skills so that you can perform the tasks that you choose to undertake in your daily life at a high level.

There are a number of techniques that you can use to build mental strength. Some of these techniques included are small one-step actions while others are multi-step processes.

The process of building mental strength takes dedication and practice. The progress and improvements that you will see in your mental toughness will take time and a significant amount of practice. The amount of mental toughness that you develop is dependent on whether you practice these techniques and focus on developing mental toughness for a specific goal with a set date such as joining the police force or becoming a professional athlete, or whether you want to hone your skills by slow and steady progression with the intention of putting them to use over a lifetime.

Take A Long Hard Look at Yourself and Evaluate Who You Are

One exercise that you can do to enhance your mental toughness is to take a good look at who you are, your values, and your beliefs and see if you are living up to those values and beliefs in your daily life. This is part of familiarizing yourself with yourself. Most people believe that they know themselves, but many are surprised to find out that they might be wrong. You may have done things a certain way for so long that you have never thought about why you are doing them; they are just habits. You could have gotten them from your parents when you were young, watching other people, television, and more. You may believe that these actions and thoughts say a lot about you and your values, but they may not say as much as you believe. This is why it is a good idea to take a long hard look at yourself and evaluate who you are. You may find out that you are a little different than you originally thought you were.

Examine things about yourself such as your personality. What are some of your character traits? What is your personality like to you? What do the people around you think of your personality? Where do the answers to the last two questions differ? Examine what emotions you need to control and what emotions you need to show more of and develop further.

Your values and beliefs
Take the time to identify and examine your core values and beliefs. What are they? Be as specific as possible and jot them down. After writing down your values and beliefs, it is a tie for you to try to access why these are your core values and beliefs. Is it because they were your parents' values and beliefs that were handed down to you? Are they the same values and beliefs that you had when you were a child? If so, do they still apply to your life today? Really take the time to think about it so that you can assess whether these values are a good thing for you to hold on to and aspire to as you try to achieve your goals.

Don't let old values and beliefs keep you from achieving your current goals. Many of the values that you had when you were younger may have been due in part to your age, the experience that you had in your life and the current state of society. You may have outgrown these values and belief, and they may no longer apply to you.

Don't let other people's values get in the way of you achieving your goals. We often have adopted values that were essentially given to us by other people. Our parents taught us their values. Some of our values were learned from our grandparents. School teachers gave us some values. We pick up some of our values from church when we were younger. These values sounded good and allowed us to fit into with the people around us but were they and are they still your values as well. It is difficult to work toward achieving values that you do not really believe in. Thus, it is very important to assess who possesses these values that we believe that we hold now.

Next, ask yourself this question: Are you living up to your values and beliefs? If the answer is no, then you need to step back for a second and figure out where the problem lies. Why are you falling short of living by your values and beliefs? The most common answer to this question is that the values and beliefs that you have identified are not truly your values and beliefs; however, they are great ideals that you believe make good values and beliefs.

Are your values in line with your goals? For instance, if you value church, Christianity, and putting out positive messages becoming a rapper is not a goal that fits with these values. When your values and your goals do not align, it is important to determine which one is more important to you and which one needs to fall back so that you can get on your way to achieving your goals or aspire to other goals. You cannot have this conundrum and effectively pursue your goal because there will be a lot of times when your values conflict with what you are asked to or need to do to succeed (unless you want to be a Christian rapper).

Develop A Belief System That is Conducive To you Achieving Your Goals

Restructure your beliefs so that they are in line with your goals. Some of your core beliefs should center around hard work and developing drive to push on and succeed. When your goals and beliefs work together and complement each other, the mental debate that would take place if they were in conflict is eliminated.

It is completely counterproductive to have a belief system that is not in line with the goals that you have set for yourself. Your belief system should push your goals forward.

Identify Your Strengths and Weaknesses

One way to build mental strength is to identify your strengths and weaknesses. Knowing your strengths and weaknesses can help you figure out where you need to improve in order to develop the mental strength that you want.

Ask others for their honest input about what your strengths and weaknesses are. Seek constructive criticism from those around you. Knowing your weaknesses will help you know where to put your focus. Since it is concerning mental strength be sure to ask questions and assess areas which are directly related to mental toughness such as emotional balance, emotional intelligence, mental clarity, drive, focus, and more.

After identifying your weaknesses, write a step by step plan to improve upon each one of these areas so that you can become stronger in these areas. Get other people's opinions as to whether you have any other weaknesses that are not listed so that you can improve upon areas in which other people around you believe that you may be falling short.

Do Not Allow Your Mental Energy to Be Wasted

Part of developing mental toughness is to develop the ability to focus and eliminate the mental clutter. Learn to differentiate between problems and issues around you that you can do something about and the ones that you cannot. Anything that you cannot do anything about should not be a focus in your mind. You need to accept these things so that you can move on to concentrate on the things that you can control and change.

Also, problems and issues of little significance should not be a focus that weighs on your mind and keeps you from doing other things. Do not concentrate on trivial things that have little to no impact on your life. This will only weigh your mind down, cutting down on the focus and the time that you can give to other things.

Avoid Being a Perfectionist

You need to do things well, and to the best of your ability in life; however, there is a line that when crossed is obsessiveness. Everything does not have to be perfect down to the last detail. Take some time to evaluate how significant the details are about a task or project that you are working on to avoid obsessively trying to be perfect. Perfection is not the key to success, it is the key to obsession, and it should be let go of in order to develop other more important things that are going on around you and in your life.

Actively Eliminate Your Negative Thoughts by Finding Positive Thoughts to Replace Them – Write Down Negative Thoughts When They Creep into Your Mind

When you are trying to accomplish a goal or simply when you are going throughout your day, negative thoughts may creep into your mind. These negative thoughts get to you, the more and more you have them, and they make you less likely to believe that you can achieve and excel at the goals that you have set for yourself.

One active step that you can take to eliminate some of your negative thoughts and their confidence draining effects is to write down your negative thought on a piece of paper. Look at the though and read over it. Is it accurate? Notice what time you experienced the thought and what brought it on. Was it talking to someone that has a negative effect on you? Was it looking at someone who you believe may be more talented than you? It is important for you to notice everything about what brought on the negative thought so that you can understand why the thought crept into your head.

Write all of the negative thoughts that you have in a day down in a journal so that you can see how many negative thoughts creep into your mind during an average day. Do this for a week so that you can notice what days of the week are the best and which are the worst. Where do you tend to be when you have negative thoughts? Maybe consider carrying a mini tape recorder with you so that you can make a note if you have a negative thought at the grocery store. After writing down all of your negative thoughts and analyzing where they come from and the basis for them, assess what type of an impact of effect the negative thought is having and will have on your performance of your daily tasks and you're achieving the goals that you set out to achieve.

Be sure to notice any patterns that may appear with negative thoughts. Are all of your negative thoughts centered around one goal? If so, this may be a sign that you should let this particular goal go. If something that you want to achieve is always causing you to have negative thoughts, evaluate why these thoughts are raised with this particular goal to see if the goal is one that is worth having.

Are your negative thoughts surrounding a person? Sometimes all of the people in our lives are not good for us and we need to take stock of how a person affects our life before we make the decision on whether or not to keep the person in our life. A toxic friend or a toxic relationship can take a toll on your emotional and mental strength and consume a significant amount of your thoughts. This is a problem that needs to be solved effectively and fast so that you can be more productive. And oftentimes, the solution is cutting the person out of our lives or keeping that person a farther distance away. If this is what it is necessary to do, then make sure that you do this in order to maintain and develop your mental and emotional strength so that you can live a productive fulfilled life.

Come up with positive thoughts to combat some of the negative thoughts that creep into your mind. Think about your strong points and the good things about you and around you that can counteract the negative thought that you are having. Make a list of these positive thoughts and keep them in a journal as well. Try to make sure that your positive thoughts always outweigh your negative ones.

Have a Ceremony to Let Go of The Past
If you often find yourself thinking about past events and occurrences in your life that have had some impact on you whether they were positive or negative, this is counterproductive and not a valuable use of your time or your mind. Still, it is often hard to let go of the past. We often stay stuck in certain moments in our past and relive them in our minds, sometimes even years later. We may dwell on or obsess about past mistakes, wishing that we could go back and change them and thinking about how great our lives would be if we could. But no matter how hard you wish that you could do something to change the past, there is no way that you can, and you have to live for today and tomorrow, not yesterday.

You may have had some negative experiences in the past that you cannot get out of your mind. You may have been mistreated in the past, perhaps you suffered some type of abuse at some point in your life. If you do not want this event to define your entire life, you have to find a way to get it to stop creeping into your mind. Identify the negative thoughts that you have internalized as a result of past events. You may want to write these down as well so that you can take a better look at them. Some of these thoughts may have to do with dealing with certain types or groups of people. Others may have to do with going to different types of events. You need to take the time to think about whether these negative thoughts and feeling that you brought with you are still valid and true today. Sometimes, if we look at our negative experiences again and really think about it, we have moved on in our lives and should be ready and willing to let the past go and start fresh in the present without all of the negatives of the past weighing us down.

If you find that the past is continuously on your mind, you may want to hold a ceremony to release yourself from the past and move into the present. This is true whether the memories in the past that are holding you back are good or bad. If you lost a relative or friend in the past, hold a celebration of life ceremony to remember the person and make a pledge to yourself to not dwell on that event of those memories again. If you were a college football player or cheerleader, have some of your teammates over for a party to reminisce; after the party is over but the memorabilia away and make a vow to move on.

Meditate and reflect on your day at the end of each day.

Each day brings new experiences with it that you can learn from and grow. In addition, there are many repeated experiences that a person has each day that he or she can improve upon. At the end of the day each day, it would be a good idea to take the time to reflect on the day that just passed and think about everything that happened, how you felt, how it affected you, why you believe that certain things occurred, and whether there is anything that you would have done differently.

Try taking about ten minutes at the end of each day to sit quietly in the back of a room, maybe play some meditation music, and strike your favorite yoga pose if you would like and reflect on the day that just occurred so that you can make an assessment of how it went and if there are things that you would do differently or change about your day to make similar days better in the future.

Practice Staying Calm in High-Pressure Situations

Practice has a way of improving the way in which we handle things. That is what it is designed to do, and when it comes to emotional toughness in high-pressure situations, practice may be the best thing that you can do to develop your mental toughness and better handle high-pressure situations.

The main key to succeeding in high-pressure situations is to stay calm and not overreact or become intimidated, but that is often much easier said than done. For example, if you are a musical performer, you can practice your music for hours and hours until you have it perfect when preparing for your first live performance in front of a large crowd. You know that you need to relax and perform the way that you rehearsed, and you are fully prepared; however, this does not guarantee that you are going to execute the performance well when you get in front of that large crowd for the first time. You may execute the performance very poorly once stage fright takes over.

In order for the performer to perform at his or her best when he or she has never done a large live performance before, the performer should practice giving performances in front of smaller crowds and work his or her way up to a larger crowd.

This strategy works well for acclimating one's self to other high-pressure situations as well. Start with lower pressure situations such as the smaller performances and gradually move towards higher and higher-pressure situations as you become more comfortable and acclimated to the pressure situation. This is similar to what organizations such as the military and NASA do with simulators. They simulate actual flight scenarios to train their pilots on how to handle real-world flights.

Additional Ways to Build Mental Toughness
There in addition to the more sophisticated ways to build your mental toughness that are some quick and easy things that you can add to your day. Here are some other interesting ways that many people have found to have an actual effect on building their mental toughness.

Cold Showers
One such way that has worked for a number of people that you may not have thought of or come across in other places is to take cold showers. Taking cold

showers can help you clear your mind and get your blood flowing and your adrenaline pumping. This can help to elevate your level of concentration and focus so that you can get on your way to achieving a goal that you set that day or having an outstanding performance.

Disconnect Yourself from Social Media
Social media is a huge phenomenon that has turned into a staple of our current culture and is here to stay. The problem with social media, however, is that it is full of tweets, blurbs, Snapchats, Instagram photos with a one-liner underneath and more tic-tacky stuff that can occupy a person's entire day with no educational or informative information being supplied. This makes it an interesting distraction; however, not something that you should be constantly utilizing throughout your day.

Constantly taking breaks to check social media or even waiting for your breaks to check social media is a distraction from what you should be doing and a break in your concentration. Unless you are actually making a significant amount of money from one of the social media channels, at which point you can consider the utilization of social media working, this is not a productive use of your time, and significant limits should be placed on your use of social media so that you can fill your mind with productive, informative, educational or insightful things.

Always Be Reading A Self-Help Book on A Subject Area in Which You Can Improve
Another way to increase your mental toughness is to expand your mind and learn new things that can improve your mental toughness, your emotional stability, your emotional intelligence and more. There are thousands of books out there on how you can improve, take control of, and master just about anything in your life. You should always be reading one of them in order to gain the information that is contained on the pages and help yourself learn how to grow and improve in this area. This is a great way to spend your free time, your lunch break, your daily commute on the subway and more. You can learn how to make friends and influence people, learn about mastery, learn the 48 laws of power, learn how to control your emotions, learn how to budget better, learn how to have more self-confidence and more by reading a book in that subject area for a few minutes a day. Constantly learning and expanding your mind is a

trait of people who possess and exhibit mental strength.

Chapter 5: Fear and Stress

Unfortunately, both fear and stress are a part of daily life. Fear is an emotion that is characterized by a feeling of intense distress to a situation which is perceived to be threatening. Stress is a biological response to an environmental condition, whether it be a threat or a physical or psychological barrier. In essence, stress is the perception that a high-pressure situation is occurring and a person's internal response to the pressure.

Both fear and stress and have a negative impact on your mental state and emotions. They can be draining on a person's energy level and ability to concentrate. These emotions can clog a person's mind if they get out of control and become the main factor that people focus on.

How Fear Affects Mental Toughness
Fear affects the mind and the emotions in a way that may be hard for some people to control or even predict. The way that you react to fear often depends on the fear stimuli, the perceived intensity of the threat and how well you react to high-pressure situations in

general. Other values such as self-preservation versus caring for others also come into play.

Fear diminishes some of the characteristics of mental toughness that are part of the unbeatable mind. If these elements of mental toughness are not fully developed in a person or the person is not able to adequately cope with the feeling of fear, some of the element of mental toughness that a person would generally count on to pull him or her out of a tough situation may not be able to be utilized at optimal levels.

Fears effects on the elements of the Unbeatable Mind and Mental Toughness
Fear can actually affect the first trait of the unbeatable mind, mental capacity if the fear is strong enough or a person is unable to handle and cope with fear properly. People who experience strong fear are often known to have breakdowns.

Even though fear diminishes the characteristics of mental strength if you do not know how to react to it properly, developing your mental toughness can actually help a person cope with and react to fear better. Mental toughness can help you react in a more productive manner to fear. The reason that there is a productive way in which people can react to fear has to do with the fact that fear is not an entirely negative emotion even though many people may initially categorize it as such. Fear is actually necessary for survival in dangerous situations. The fear emotion warns a person that there is a great danger ahead.

Although fear is not entirely a negative emotion, as it does serve to warn you of danger, it is an emotion that can stop you from pursuing and achieving your goals. Fear can keep you from doing the things that you want to do in life. Thus, it is crucial for you to be able to handle fear properly in order to get the things done that you would like to get done in your life or participate in the activities in which you would like to participate. For instance, you may want to participate in a sport like football; however, you have a significant fear of being injured. If you focus on your fear and do not handle it properly, you may choose not to play football, and you will miss out on participating in something that you really wanted to do.

Stress Causes: **Mental Toughness Causes:**

	With practice immersing one's self into a high-pressure situation, a person can stay calm under pressure.
A feeling of being overwhelmed.	Time management skills.

How Stress Affects Mental Toughness

There are some causes of stress that are common to everyone according to polls and studies. These common causes of stress include job and workplace stress, financial stress, stress over personal relationships, stress over daily hassles, stress from having too many things to do and too little time, and stress over family and children. Stress is a part of daily life that is unavoidable. However, we all know that stress has a very negative effect on the body. It is an emotion that can heighten performances in some and lead to an emotional breakdown in other people.

Unlike fear which tends to be caused by something that scares a person in some way, stress is caused by being worried about something, whether it be something that scares you or not. There are some things that traditionally tend to cause a person to feel stressed. One of the primary causes of stress is being under a lot of pressure.

A significant amount of pressure can cause a person to feel a great deal of stress. This pressure may be caused by having a lot of things to do at work, too many family obligations, having to perform in a sporting event, having too much to do and feeling that you do not have a lot of time to get it all done and more. When you are under a significant amount of pressure and thus stressed out, your mind is filled with thoughts of whatever is stressing you out making it hard to concentrate and think as clearly as you would have if you were more relaxed. This affects the mental toughness or strength that you currently possess because you may see that the positive traits of mental strength diminish in these situations if you have not trained yourself to handle stress.

Something else that may trigger stress and thus affect mental strength is emotional things. Things which are emotional include relationships with spouses, friends, family, and others around you, the inability to find a job, the need for more money and wondering where and how you are going to get it and more. Although some of these stressors are mental as well, they tend to be very emotional. If you have not developed your emotional intelligence, you may become overrun by your emotions, thus losing mental strength. We have all seen this happen to someone; a person seems to have it all together, seems to be very smart, has a good job, and is highly functional until he or she is going through a breakup or a divorce and that person seems to start to unravel. If you are not equipped with the emotional intelligence and mental toughness to handle emotionally stressing situations, you may become too stressed out to function at your normal level.

Another common cause of stress is facing significant changes in your life. This may start to seem overwhelming to you and cause you to fail to react in your normal way, fail to think things through in a logical manner, or otherwise fail to do everything that you need to do for these changes to go smoothly. This can cause you to question whether or not you are mentally fit to go through these changes. You may start to believe, especially at times when things start to seem more difficult, that you were only mentally strong enough for the way your life was before the changes and even start to resist change or want things to change back to the way that they were. If you have trained yourself to have the mental strength to cope with this type of situation, it will go more smoothly, and you may even enjoy the significant changes that come in your life.

Feeling a lack of control over the things that take place around you, or your life, in general, can cause you to feel significantly stressed out. You may believe that you do not know what to expect in life and that nothing you do seems to have a significant impact on the way that things turn out for you. All of the preparation and the planning that you do seems to be for nothing. This type of stress can diminish your resolve, affect your ability to set goals, your willpower and more due to the fact that you may fail to see the point of doing these things.

There are certain times in your life when things are uncertain. You do not know what is going to happen. You may be worried about the future or even what is going to take place in the present. These are the times when stress tends to form and build up. This undoubtedly affects how you are able to function and your thought processes.

The problem with stress is that it does not just include the mental emotion of feeling tense or anxious or the inability to concentrate as well as you should. Many people have a strong physical reaction to stress, and you could be one of them. Stress causes the human body to experience a number of negative health consequences. Some of these reactions are minor, and some are more severe. If a person is under stress for a significant period of time and does not take the time to address the issue properly, this can take a major toll on the person's health.

Some significant changes can occur in your body due to high-stress levels and some significant health problems that can result. This is the primary reason that it is important to manage stress properly. Some of the most common effect that stress has on your body include headaches, fatigue, problems falling asleep and staying asleep, muscle pain and tense muscles, nausea. Mentally stress can cause an inability to focus, lack of motivation, a feeling of being overwhelmed, depression, irritability restlessness and more. The most severe effects of unregulated stress over a long period of time are high blood pressure, obesity heart disease, and diabetes. Stress can also lead to some negative coping behaviors which compound the health problems that it can cause. Some of the negative coping strategies that stress produces include the use of alcohol and tobacco as well as the use and abuse of prescription and illegal drugs. It can also lead to overeating as a person tries to consume comfort food and may neglect to eat a proper diet. Withdrawn from social interaction is another result of being under too much pressure and stress.

You have probably heard of a type A personality; this is the type of personality that business executives and the like tend to have. They are under stress a lot and tend to develop health problems as a result if they do not find proper outlets to cope with stress.

Use Mental Toughness to Deal with Fear and Stress

Yes, you can use mental toughness to better deal with fear and stress. Mental toughness addresses some of the underlying causes of both fear and stress. Addressing the underlying issues is one of the primary ways that you want to handle these two emotions so that you can mitigate them.

Mental toughness and developing your mental strength can help a person react to fear in a more positive manner that makes the experience of fearless detrimental to the person and even allows the person to think strategically in order to get through the fear-filled situation. Fear is a state of mind that can be altered. It is not just your reaction to fear but also whether and how much fear you feel in all a part of your mind and your emotions.

Moreover, both the amount of stress that you feel and the way that you handle the stress that you do feel can be altered with mental toughness training. Training your mind to help you stay calm in high-pressure situations and taking steps to become more responsible can affect how much stress you feel. The way that you handle stress can be altered by the plan that you develop to handle the underlying situation as well as the calming techniques that you use.

Perception
Developing your mental toughness can help you deal with stress because the amount of stress that you feel in a situation often depends on certain variables. One of these variables is the way that you perceive the

situation that is the central cause of the stress or from which the stressor is arising. The way that you perceive a situation may have to do with past experiences. Past experiences can include your own past experiences with a given situation as well as past experiences watching a parent, older sibling, family member, or someone else deals with the same situation.

Another factor that ways into how you perceive a situation is your self-esteem. A person with lower self-esteem may become more stressed out when thinking about relocating to a new area or getting a new job because he or she may wonder how he is going to meet and fit in with new people. Your level of self-esteem can be elevated with emotional intelligence training, a subject which is discussed in the last chapter of this book.

Yet, another factor that goes into how you perceive a situation is how you tend to perceive things in general. Do you tend to perceive things more positively or negatively? Are you a positive or a negative person? If you typically have a lot of negative thoughts that you tend to leave unchecked, this could have a significant impact on the way you perceive the situations that arise and how stressed out you become as a result of these situations. One of the common traits that people with mental toughness display is a propensity to think positively and to see the upside about a given situation. Furthermore, as discussed in the chapter concerning Ways to Develop Mental Strength, you should identify your negative thoughts, address why you have formed those thoughts and whether they are accurate or inaccurate, and actively combat these thoughts with more positive thoughts.

Perspective

Perspective is pretty close to perception, but it differs slightly. Perspective has to do with the angle at which you are looking at things. You have surely heard the phrase "try to keep things in perspective." This means that the lens through which you look at an event or situation should be in focus so that it does not magnify it to the point that it is no longer in perspective. You need to be able to judge things that occur for the significance that they actually have. You need to not place too much importance on things that do not have an equal amount of significance. Developing mental toughness can help you put things into perspective and keep them in perspective. Putting things in the proper perspective comes from mental competency as well as emotional intelligence and emotional balance.

Your Experience with The Pressure Situation

Your own experience with a particular pressure situation has a significant impact on the amount of stress and fear that you experience when facing that situation. Let's say, for instance, you are a college basketball player playing in a game, and you have been fouled. The stands are full, and the game is televised. If this is your first game, you may experience a sudden pang of fear when thinking about how you are going to execute the foul shot and you may have been stressed out about the game all week. However, if you are into your junior year and you play regularly, the fear that you used to feel during your freshman season may have subsided and the amount of stress that the impending game caused you all week may be virtually non-existent.

One key way to develop mental toughness when handling a stressful situation such as the one described above is to immerse yourself in a stressful situation starting with situations that are a lower level of stress and increase the pressure until you get to the higher level of pressure which is the game. This will help you to curb your fear, and the amount of stress that this situation causes you to experience will be less than it would if you had not taken this step. In addition, repeated practicing is the key to being comfortable in a given situation. This applies not only to sports but to most other areas of life as well.

Another example of how your personal experiences affect how much stress you feel in a given situation and how much fear it brings on is that of the end of a relationship. If you have been in relationships before and they always ended with a breakup, some of the things that lead to the break up may still be in the back of your mind as well as the feelings of loss that you felt from the break up itself. You may bring these feelings and experiences into a new relationship, and this may affect what you feel, thus bringing pressure and stress in the new relationship. You may even fear breaking up with may cause you to be more passive and less self-assured. This may be a change from the behavior that you displayed in your previous relationships in which you may have displayed more confidence and were less timid. You may have tried to force things to fit less and felt more secure about the relationship as a whole. Because your previous experiences with relationships were negative in that they always ended with breakups, you needed to have dealt with your emotions as a result of these experiences properly including honing your emotional intelligence skills to be more in tune with your partner. This is a topic that is cover in more detail in the last chapter of this book.

Other Pressures

The amount of stress that you feel over a given situation is also controlled by the amount of stress that you are under in general. If you have a lot of responsibilities and you are having a difficult time fitting them all in and managing your time, this can cause you to feel a great deal of stress and even fear. Thus, your perception of a specific situation does not have to be the things upon which the stress is based, and which triggers the feeling of fear. Every situation that you are dealing with right then can compound themselves into a giant stressful situation if you do not take the effective steps in trying to handle each situation as it arises. This is where the discipline and willpower that is developed when practicing and developing mental toughness come in.

Addressing issues in the appropriate amount of time can keep things from spiraling out of control and minimize that amount that you have on your plate at one time. The importance of this cannot be underestimated because you may look back at the situation later and realize that none of the individual issues would have caused so much stress and fear if they had been addressed and handled alone but because they were not, these issues snowballed into what seemed like an impending catastrophe which can cause great fear and stress that should have been avoided with proper planning.

Your Emotional Stability
Your emotional stability has a great deal to do with how much stress you experience. People who are overly emotional or who have less control over their emotions may find themselves experiencing a great deal of stress whereas people who have more control over their emotions may find the situations that the other person found stressful to be moderately easy situations to handle.

If you've experienced a similar situation in the past and your emotions are still raw, or you've experienced a significant amount of negative emotion about that situation in the past, this can have a significant effect on the amount of stress that experience due to that situation. In fact, if your emotions alone can have a huge impact on your perception of whether or not something is a stressful situation or one that evolves fear. Thus, emotional intelligence training is very significant in this type of situation. You need to get in touch with your own emotions as well as learn to assess and identify the triggers for these emotions so that you know where they are coming from and where they originate. Making strides in your level of emotional stability will allow you to experience less stress and fear in many situations as well as handle these emotions better.

Your Values

Your values also play a key role in how much stress you will experience in a given situation, the solutions that you come up with to handle it and the amount of fear that both the problem and the solution cause. This is because your values decide what is important to you and it is what you deem to be important that determines whether you fear losing it or stress out about it. For example, a law school student who places high importance on getting good grades on his exams so that he can get a job at a top-notch law firm would be stressed out if he did not have time to study. A student in the same class that is more interested in doing community service work and does not care about grades, only passing would stress out a lot less over the same situation. Worrying about grades is only in line with the first student's values and not the values of the second student. Thus, the same situation cannot evoke the same amount of stress in both students.

Because values are so central to the amount of stress that you experience, you should examine your values and alter them in a way that will allow you to feel less stress and handle things properly. If you value money and you are constantly stressing out over when you will have money and whether or not you will have enough money, maybe you should examine whether money should be one of your values. Constantly stressing out about money suggests that your aspirations for money are not leading to happiness; instead, your aspiration for money is leading to unhappiness. Try lowering money a little on your value list and find solutions to make ends meet with the amount of money that you already have. You may want to try downsizing or budgeting better to satisfy your money needs instead of trying to obtain more money.

This is why it is important to set relevant goals (remember SMART goals), to ensure that your goals are relevant to your present and your future. Likewise, your goals should be attainable. You should not go around chasing goals and dreams that you cannot seem to ever catch; especially if there is a good chance that you never will. It is also important to assess your values to ensure that they truly are and should be the things that you value. In addition, the use of mentally strong traits such as willpower can help you take steps to stick to goals that are in line with the values that really matter to you.

Your Support System
Your personal support system is critical to the amount of stress and fear that you feel in a given situation. Thus, this is one of the most significant factors in determining how much stress and fear you experience. A person with a strong support system may feel little to no stress in situations in which a person with a weak support system would get stressed out. One of the primary examples of this is when a person is stressing out about money. A person with a significant support system which includes parents, siblings, and friends from whom the person can borrow money would not stress out nearly as much as a person who has to try to make ends meet on his or her own. The first person may try too keep his or her finances in order and to make sure he always has the money for rent and the car note; however, the second person must make sure that he or she succeeds in always having the money for

rent and the car note. There is much less room for error and a potential for a far more stressful situation to form with the second person that there is with the first person due to the inadequate support system that the second person has.

Another example of how your support system factors in is with the above example of a breakup. A person with a strong support system may bounce back more quickly due to friends and relatives being supportive of the person and spending time with him or her. The amount of loss is minimized in this instance because there was a strong enough support system that the person does not feel a significant void in his or her life. This can also result in the person being less fearful of a breakup. People with an adequate support system may be more likely to let a relationship go if it is not working out and move on.

Building a strong support system is part of developing your mental strength. This is because the people that you have around you impact your thoughts, attitudes, beliefs, and values, People who exhibit mental toughness often choose to be around other people who have this type of mental training. They are positive people who tend not to bring them down or hold them back in life because part of developing mental strength is recognizing the type of people that do hold you back. Use emotional intelligence skills to assess the people around you and make sure that they are the type of people that you should be around. Eliminating people from your life is tough; however, it is often necessary to get rid of negative vibes and influences in your life.

Your Amount of Discipline
There are some positive coping strategies for dealing with stress, but they take discipline. Thus, you must develop this mental strength skill in order to handle stress properly. One of these positive coping strategies to reduce stress properly is through regular exercise. Exercise is a healthy way to release some stress and anger while burning calories and keeping in shape. Another positive technique to release stress positively is to make sure that you have time for the things that you enjoy such as hobbies and past times away from work and taking care of responsibilities. This requires proper time management. Spending time with friends and family is yet another way to relieve stress healthily. Relaxation techniques can also help reduce the amount of stress that you are feeling, as well as your level of irritability while keeping your blood pressure and heart rate normal. Some relaxation techniques include

yoga, deep breathing, meditation, massages, and tai chi.

Chapter 6: Setting Goals

Goal setting is an important component of accomplishing the things that you want to accomplish in life. To be productive and accomplish goals you must first clearly identify the goal that you would like to accomplish. It is important for these goals to be as clearly defined as possible and not vague or ambiguous. Clearly defining the goal helps to put you in the mindset to accomplish this goal.

Mental toughness directly applies to goal setting. As stated earlier, people with significant mental strength set goals, often in a series, starting with the easiest and quickest goal to accomplish and moving on to more and more complex goals.

Key elements to goal setting.
1) **Make sure that the goals that you set are goals that you are motivated to achieve.**

One of the best ways to accomplish goals is to set goals that you really want to accomplish. Goals that you are excited about and look forward to starting and completing are goals that you are more likely to stick to and accomplish.

This may seem easier said than done with some goals because often you must set goals for completing homework, school work, or work which may not truly excite you. However, it is still important to find and identify a motivating force behind the goal so that you will strive to achieve it. The motivating force could be getting a weekend off to do something that you really love or getting the raise that you wanted. Either way, both the goal and the motivation behind the goal should be very clear and specific in order to encourage yourself to complete the goal.

2) Write your goal down and inform people about it.

After you have clearly identified your goals and the motivation behind clearly, you need to neatly write them down or print them out and post them on the wall. You need your goals to be displayed concretely so that you cannot brush them under the rug and forget about them.

Furthermore, you should let your friends and family know what your goals are so that they are now 'publicized' in your world. This will help you stick to your goals because telling people about them makes them more real. After you have told the people around you about your goals, it becomes harder to put them off or deviate from them due to lack of willpower, a belief that the goals that you have set are not urgent or other reasons. Friends and family can encourage you to stick to your goals. They are a great source of emotional support that will aid you when you want to achieve something. They can often help you out on the way to achieving your goals and remind you of what they are.

Another way that friends, family, and the people around you encourage you to stick to your goals is that once they are announced, there is a sort of shame in going back on your word. Not sticking to your goals after telling people about them may make you seem flaky and cause people not to take you as seriously in other aspects of your life. It will seem as though you cannot keep your word, even if it is only to yourself. Part of the reason that telling people about your goals is included is because once you tell people that you are going to do something, it is best that you actually stick to it and do it.

3) Set SMART goals.

S (Specific)	Goals need to be as specific as possible.
M (Measurable)	Goals need to be measurable.
A (Attainable)	Goals need to be attainable by *you*.
R (Relevant)	Goals need to be relevant to you.
T (Time-Bound)	Goals need to have specific time constraints set on them.

All of the MBA programs and many articles about goal setting today are talking about setting SMART goals. SMART is an acronym which makes all of the parts that the goal must include easier to remember. SMART stands for S) Specific Goals, M) Measurable Goals, A) Attainable Goals, R) Relevant Goals, and T) Time-Bound Goals.

S) Specific Goals

According to the SMART goals philosophy and as mentioned above, the goals that you set should be as specific as possible. Make sure that the goals that you set are as specific as possible. This means that you should not leave any significant questions concerning exactly what your goal is open for debate, discussion or confusion. It is very important that you fully flesh out your goals so that you can understand what they are and what you need to do to achieve them.

The main problem with not specifically detailing your goal is that you may not be exactly sure of what you want to do. This uncertainty lends itself more to being termed a wish than a goal because it is not specific enough to be noted as a goal.

Making your goals as specific as possible allows you to think about in advance whether or not this was the true end goal. This is very important because oftentimes the answer is no, and the goal needs to be changed slightly or maybe even significantly for you to ultimately get what you what after you achieve your goal. I'm am sure you have heard the saying "Be careful what you wish for, you just might get it," detailing your specific goal can lessen the changes that what you wished for wasn't really what you wanted.

M) Measurable Goals

The goals that you set should be measurable, meaning that there is a specific amount, date, or length of time in which the goal needs to be accomplished. Do not leave the goal vague as to amounts and things of that nature because these values may soon start to decrease. If you first wanted to save up $5000, and you don't write down the exact amount of money that you wanted to save, this value may soon decrease to $3000 when you get tired of working and it starts to take you a little longer than you thought that it would and not be as easy as you thought that it would be to save up the money. This is where mental toughness comes into play. If you set a specific and measurable goal, you can use some of the tips included in this book to

A) Attainable Goals

It is important for the goals that you set to be attainable *by you*. Although you want to strive to achieve as much as you can, it does you very little good to set goals which are impossible to achieve. This is a waste of time and will only lead to frustration. Instead, when identifying the goal with specificity, make sure that all of the specific parts of the goal are attainable. You need to be qualified to achieve each part of the goal.

Everybody wants to accomplish such a great feat in life or to be notable and standout in some way. You can stand out more by accomplishing what you set out to accomplish that by setting a goal that was so out of reach that you never can achieve it. Goals should not be so easy and simple that you don't have to work for them or that you should have expected to achieve them rather easily; however, they should not be entirely too difficult to achieve either.

R) Relevant Goals

All of your goals should apply to things that you actually want to accomplish and that benefit you. At first, you may assume that since you are the one who is setting the goal, this would automatically be true; however, it is not a given. This is because people often get their ideas from somewhere or someone else. For instance, when setting goals for your New Year's resolutions, many people may select some common and popular resolutions that seem like positive things to aim for, however, these resolutions may not have been something that the person actually interested in, *they only thought that they were*. Common goals which are positive in nature and seem like goals for which you should aspire to, are not the same as goals that you actually do aspire to.

Your goals should be relevant to you at the time and place you are now in your life and taking into account where you would like to be in the future. One mistake that people make when they fail to reexamine their goals every so often is that their goals may be relevant to them; however, they apply to how the person was in the past. Thus, goals need to be relevant to both *you* and *now*.

    T) Time-Bound Goals
Goals should be time-bound. The best way to encourage yourself to start on a goal is to set a deadline. This deadline needs to be concrete in order to encourage you to keep moving on the way to your goal. Set a deadline that is realistic but does show some sense of urgency.

Goals with no time limit are goals that you may take forever to complete. This is because there is no sense of urgency and you can always justify putting them off while telling yourself that you are sticking to your goals and that you are focused and determined to succeed and achieve them. This is because it is difficult to not still be on course to achieve a goal that you have an infinite amount of time to fulfill. You can always keep telling yourself that you will start on the goal tomorrow.

4. Move goals into action with an action plan. Devising an action plan for your goals is the best way to move them from simple aspirations to things that you are actively trying to accomplish. After identifying the goal with specificity, you will need to identify each step along the way to achieving your goal. You may want to group the steps into subheading categories but be sure to list every single thing that you need to do to get to your goal. When you break the end goal into smaller steps, each small step is easier to achieve and does not take as much time, energy, and determination as the larger goal itself; thus, these smaller steps are easier to handle and make the larger goals seem less intimidating and more doable.

5. Incorporate your goals into your daily routine.

Identify a part of your goal that you can do everyday so that each day you are at least taking one small step toward your goal every day. This is a great way to not only break your goal up into small and accomplishable parts; it is a way to make your goal a part of your daily routine. It is much harder to put the goal off or forget about it if it is part of your every day routine. Furthermore, it will seem as if it takes less willpower to get to your goal.

Goals and mental toughness

Developing some of the common traits of mental strength can help you set and achieve your goals. The first trait of mentally strong people that will help you along the way to achieving your goals is mental competency. Ensuring that you are mentally competent can make sure that your goals are realistic and help you to put the importance of these goals into perspective.

Other traits such as resilience, willpower, emotional intelligence, having a winner's mind, possessing the ability to focus, surrounding yourself with mentally strong people, and avoiding bucking the system too often all work together to help a person achieve his or her goals. All of these characteristics are necessary to possess and cultivate if you want to attain higher and higher levels of achievement.

Chapter 7: Emotional Intelligence

What Is Emotional Intelligence?

Emotional intelligence is the ability to recognize and understand your own emotions as well as the emotions of others. It has a variety of different definitions with no one definition being superior to the others. Some texts define emotional intelligence as having four fundamental parts which include: managing emotions, perceiving emotions, understanding emotions, and using emotions. Other texts consider emotional intelligence to be self-awareness, social awareness, relationship management, self-management, and emotional intelligence. Still more consider emotional intelligence to be composed of five parts; these five parts are social skills, self-awareness, self-regulation, motivation, and empathy. One thing that is agreed upon is that emotional intelligence consists of being both aware of your own self and your emotions as well as being conscious of the people around you and their emotions.

Emotional intelligence gives you the ability to differentiate between different emotions that you may experience and identify and label each one correctly.

This skill is a very important skill for people to possess because understanding your own emotions and being able to differentiate between them gives you the opportunity to control your emotions and take steps to adjust them. For instance, if you notice that a given thing makes you depressed, you can take steps to counter that in advance to avoid or minimize this emotional response.

Understanding and being able to differentiate between the emotions, responses, and behaviors of others allows you to interact better with other people. This is very important because a great deal of our lives has to do with interaction with other people. You can benefit from this in almost every facet of your life. A salesman can understand body language, and facial expressions, and understands which statements a person may take offense.

The Ability to Listen to Your Emotions

Emotional intelligence is also the ability to listen to and adjust your thinking and behavior based on the information that your emotions are giving you.

For it to be a good idea, however, for you to listen to your emotions and be guided by them, you need to have the ability to keep your emotions in balance.

Your emotions need to be under control before it is okay to listen to them. It would not be wise for an overly emotional person to listen to and be guided by his or her emotions. Thus, you must be able first to identify your emotions, and then understand where your emotions are coming from and what triggers them. Is it an event from the past? Is it negative thoughts about your worthiness? Is it an overly inflated ego? It is important to understand whether your emotions are coming from the event or person that you are dealing with or something else before you judge your reaction.

Your emotions need to provide you with accurate information in order for you to be able to use them in a manner that is beneficial to you. Thus, you need to be in tune with your emotions and tune them up from time to time so that the information that they are presenting to you is useful and accurate and thus a good guide for your behavior.

Why Do You Need Emotional Intelligence?

Everyone *needs* to have emotional intelligence, and it can definitely make your life easier if you have a great deal of emotional intelligence. The ability to understand the way that others are thinking, feeling and may react as well as being in touch with your own emotions that are formed for the situations that are in can help you navigate through situations in daily life far more effectively and with greater ease than you would if you lacked this skill.

It is important for a person to understand how his or her emotions connect to his or her behavior. Emotions have a significant effect on how a person perceives things, and in turn how he or she reacts to it. If you do not understand and are not in control of your emotions, you may not understand the reason for your reaction. Many people never even bother to think about why they react a certain way to certain things. Your behavior directly relates to your reaction to certain stimuli.

Furthermore, the way in which other people react and behave toward you is directly correlated to the emotions that they feel when they are around you as well. So, it is best to be in tune to the so that you can do well. In fact, people with a high degree of emotional intelligence often manipulate other people's emotions to tilt situations in their favor.

When Do You Need Emotional Intelligence?

There are a significant number of situations in life when you need to have emotional intelligence so it would be wise to think that it is always good to have and utilize emotional intelligence. In fact, it can be argued that the only time that you do not need to have emotional intelligence is when you are sleeping...alone. This is because life is filled with interactions between other people and these interactions often involve emotions.

In Relationships
One of the most obvious times in which you can benefit from having emotional intelligence is in your personal relationships. Relationships are often filled with and even based on emotions.

Knowing when your spouse or significant other is happy, upset, or annoyed can help your relationship run a lot smoother, so does knowing the right thing to say and when to say it. Awkward people, people without adequate people skills often have a difficult time meeting people and thus forming relationships. If you have no clue what to say to the opposite sex, when or what they may find offensive, you may have a difficult time finding a mate, most cases are not this extreme, and most people do have some emotional intelligence; however, improving your emotional intelligence can help you to enjoy your relationships more, form more relationships and closer bonds with other people, feel less intimidated in social situations and network better with others.

At Work

Although it may not seem as though emotional intelligence comes into play as much at work, if there are other people around you at work, and these people are likely to experience emotions, then emotional intelligence can be a great asset to you in the workplace. In fact, emotional intelligence can help your workday go more smoothly, help you to get along with your coworkers better, get the people around you to look more favorably upon your ability to do your work and even get you a raise or a promotion that you have wanted for a long time.

The first time you use emotional intelligence at work is at the job interview itself. Since the interviewer may be seeing a number of different candidates, you do not only want to make sure that you impress him or her with your credentials and impressive resume, you also want to make sure that you do not rub the person the wrong way. Yes, catering to your interviewer's emotions is important if you want to land that job.

You know you need to be able to read signals and take hints in order to secure the position. But what does taking hints involve? Taking hints and reading signals involves identifying the emotions of the interviewer and acting according to what is pleasing to him or her. Or, it may mean realizing that this is not a person that you want to work with and that you need to look for another job. Either way, it is important for you to be in tune with the thoughts and feelings of the interviewer so that you can perform well or make a judgement call as to whether this is an environment that you can work in.

Emotional Intelligence versus Intellectual Intelligence

When looking at the benefits of having emotional intelligence, one has to wonder which one is better to possess, emotional intelligence or intellectual intelligence. Intellectual intelligence is a test of someone's academic intelligence and is often measured by standardized tests. Intellectual intelligence gauges your ability to learn and understand information that is being presented to you. In addition, it is representative of your logical reasoning ability, reading comprehension skills and often reading and math skills as well. This type of intelligence is very beneficial to have in the workplace and is often an indicator of who will perform well at the tasks assigned and shine at his or her job.

How to Gain Emotional Intelligence

Emotional intelligence is important to have since so much of life is spent dealing with other people, and you also need to understand your own emotions in order to be successful and enjooy your life. Some people may be blessed with emotional intelligence already, and these people may know who they are. They are the ones who are always making friends and have an easy time with people. Even still, they may not have developed their emotional intelligence skills in all situations and environments. A person can have a high level of emotional intelligence with their friends but a very low level of emotional intelligence at work. This can come from feeling connected to friends and taking the time to listen and emphasize while, at the same time, feeling disconnected at work and not making the same effort to understand the emotions of others and interact with them well. This type of person can benefit from learning how to gain emotional intelligence as it applies to different situations.

Other people may have a more difficult time around people and fail to make friends easily. They may also have trouble relating to people at work. They may even experience some anxiety when they are in situations where they are meeting people for the first time. If you are one of these people, you probably already believe that you need some extra help when dealing with other people and trying to understand how to better interact with them. You simply may not have been aware that increasing your emotional intelligence can help you do this.

Here are some ways that you can improve upon your emotional intelligence:

1) Get in touch with your own emotions by taking time to reflect on them.

Emotional intelligence involves not only understanding the emotions of others; it also involves getting in touch with your own emotions as well. This is important when interacting with others because the way people think, feel and act towards you may be significant in the way you interact with them. It is also significant to how you perceive the experience no matter how it goes.

Because it is so important to understand your emotions in different situations, you need to get in touch with your emotions and the best way to do this is by taking the time to think about them actively. Reflect on your emotions through the day at the end of the day. Jot down the emotions that you experienced in different situations, how you felt, whether or not you enjoyed it. Did something make you nervous? Did you experience fear?

Understanding what emotions you experience in different situations can allow you to gain better control over your emotions. This is especially true if you are a person who experiences anger issues. Determining exactly what type of events may trigger anger in you will help you to control it better.

2) Solicit the opinions of others.
When assessing emotions and trying to gain a great understanding of how yourself and others think and feel, it is important to get other people's opinions. This is because another person may view

a situation differently than you do and may experience different emotions in the same situation. Another person may even offer you a different way for you to look at a situation that is troubling you or you have not figured out how to handle on your own.

Ask as many questions as you can about different situations and scenarios that you face and interactions that you have so that you can gain the most accurate insight into how the other people involved and even the people watching think and feel about the situation.

3) Stop and think before doing some things or having some interactions

Normally, we go through our day doing the things we need to do and interacting with the people that we need to interact with without thinking about it first. Take a moment to stop and think about some of these things before you do them and some interactions before you have them. As yourself what do you expect to feel about doing this? How would you feel if you did not do it today? How do you think that this interaction is going to go? Do you think that you will enjoy the interaction? Are you dreading it?

After taking the time to stop and think and asking yourself some of the questions listed above, you may want to jot the answers down on a piece of paper and slip it in your pocket.

After the event or interaction takes place, think about whether it went the way you expected and whether it went differently because you stopped and thought about it. Answering the first question will help you to understand how closely your expectations about the event or interaction coincided with the actual occurrence. After doing this a few times you may be able to see where your perception is off and start bringing your expectations beforehand and the actual occurrence closer to matching. Answering the second question, 'Do you believe that the event or interaction went the same way or that it went different from what it would have if you had not stopped and thought about the situation first?' can help you understand whether you need to take the time out to think about your actions, thoughts, and interactions before you have the to make sure that you are in control of your emotion and react the best way that you possibly can to the situation.

4) Observe and study the emotions and interactions of others.

To learn more about how other people experience emotions and how they think and react to things, it is a good idea to simply watch them for a while so that you can see for yourself how they experience certain situations.

Maybe go to a local park or a shopping mall, sit on the bench and simply watch people when they walk by. How do people seem to treat each other? Are people who do not know each other polite to each other?

Jot down so notes about some of the things that you see. Especially note the reactions that you did not expect and maybe hypothesize as to why your opinion of what the reaction would be was wrong.

5) Practice putting yourself in situations which may help to improve your interactions with others and your ability to understand their emotions.

If you are uncomfortable meeting people, you should not try to avoid such situations. On the contrary, you should go to as many of these types of events and place yourself in as many of these situations as possible until you get better at it. (Important Note: If you really need practice in this area, it may be best to start off in some places where you do not have to worry about seeing the people again. Try and out of state conference for a hobby or interest of yours and see how you do at mixing and mingling. Or try going to a nightclub or bar in a neighboring city, mingling and asking someone to dance with you. You can even stay at a hotel overnight and think about your experience.

The more experience you gain in certain situations, the better you will become at understanding them and handling them with poise ease and grace. So, go out there and practice interacting and take notes to see how this improves your level of emotional intelligence. Practicing certain situations which you find socially challenging is also part of developing mental toughness, the ability to endure and succeed in the given situation through practice and perseverance. And take notes!

6) Learn to handle criticism well and even learn from it.

Sometimes, as you go throughout your day something that you have done or said may receive some criticism from someone else. Do take this personally. On the contrary, try to learn to handle criticism, so long as it is not too harsh, in a constructive manner. Ask the person who gives the criticism of what he or she saw wrong with the situation that led up to the criticism. If there really is a flaw of some sort, this gives you the opportunity to fix it. And even if you do not agree with the criticism, you get to hear the other person's thoughts and feelings on the matter which leads to an improvement in your level of emotional intelligence.

The Negative Effects of Not Having Emotional Intelligence

There are a number of negative effects of not having emotional intelligence. In fact, if you lack emotional intelligence, you are probably experiencing the negative effects and may even know what they are.

People who do not have emotional intelligence struggle when dealing with other people, some may not even realize it. Emotional intelligence is often referred to as people skills. People with poor people skills tend to misread situations and may say things that are inappropriate or even offensive due to the fact that they have a lowered ability to read other people.

As stated earlier in this book, empathy, or the ability to empathize with others is a trait that a person needs in order to have a higher level of emotional intelligence and form significant connections to others. Without the ability to place one's self in another person's shoes and understand how he or she feels, a person can only relate to situations from his or her own perspective. This is similar to 'going in blind.' This type of person can get some things right, but he or she would get a great deal wrong due to the fact that he is only speaking from his own perspective.

There are certain signs that a person may have a low level of emotional intelligence. These signs tend to illustrate a failure to understand and relate to how other people feel.
    1) Getting into frequent arguments
When you do not have the emotional intelligence to communicate well with others, oftentimes, this can result in your communications becoming contentious.

This is because positive communications often break down when one of the parties in the conversation is insensitive, condescending, arrogant, selfish or displays other negative characteristics that may frustrate, annoy, or anger the person with whom he or she is conversing, and this may often escalate into an argument.

    2) Feeling a lot of negative emotions

Emotional intelligence is not just the awareness of the feelings of others; it includes self-awareness as well. Therefore, if you are feeling a lot of negative emotions, you may not be in touch with your emotions and what is causing you to feel this way. People with higher amounts of emotional intelligence tend not to let a lot of negative emotions linger. They seek to find out what is causing these emotions and try to address them so that they can experience more positive emotions and less negative emotions.

    3) Overly negative perceptions of other people and situations

Poor emotional intelligence can lead to not only negative feelings and emotions but also overly negative perceptions of situations which other people may not have viewed as poorly. Failure to be able to connect to people can lead to you seeing more negatively than people who have the emotional and social skills to make a connection.

4) Behavioral Issues

Some people who have low emotional intelligence actually develop behavioral issues as a result of not knowing exactly how to handle their negative emotions. Negative emotions which are not addressed and remedied to some extent often aggravate things and can lead a person to develop frustration and anger which often manifests itself as behavioral issues.

5) Lower Performance

When you are dealing with unresolved emotional issues which result from a lower level of emotional intelligence, this may often result in lower performance. Emotional issues cloud your mind and your judgement causing you to be able to concentrate less on your work. In addition, these issues could be the elephant in the room in a workspace if this is where the emotional issues originate.

6) Lower Level of Self Confidence

When you do not know how to relate to other people, this can result in a lower level of self-confidence. The fact that things tend not to go smoothly, and problems tend to originate when dealing with other people can weigh on a person's self-esteem until it starts to diminish.

7) Refusing to Listen to the Opinions of Others and Their Point of View

People who have lower levels of emotional intelligence often have narcissistic personality disorders that cause them to believe that their thoughts and opinions are superior to that of others. You have probably met this type of person who tends to be loud, rude, and wrong. It is hard for this person to understand that there can be another way of thinking about things that differ from the way that he or she thinks about it.

8) Blames Other People for His or Her Own Mistakes

Everyone has met someone who has someone else to blames for everything that goes wrong around him or her. This person barely takes responsibility for his or her own actions if something goes wrong. Part of mental toughness is feeling as if you can control a situation; therefore, people who have developed their mental toughness and emotional intelligence tend to take more responsibility for the mistakes that are made.

9) Find it Hard to Develop and Maintain Close Relationships

Close relationships are important to develop and maintain; however, they take a good deal of emotional intelligence to do so. Close relationships tend to require that one person empathize with the other, take responsibility for his own actions, listen to the other person's thoughts and opinions, and understand how the other person may feel in given situations.

Just as there are traits that people with a significant amount of emotional intelligence display, people with insufficient degrees of emotional intelligence tend to display some common traits as well. These traits are, of course, negative in nature and result from a lack of understanding or caring about other people. Part of developing mental toughness includes developing emotional intelligence which can benefit a person in many facets of daily life and help minimize these negative traits.

Conclusion

Almost everything that you want to do and is worth doing in life takes some degree of mental toughness. With is the determination to push forward and surmount hurdles, stay organized and motivated, use willpower and resilience to keep moving forward toward the goals and dreams that you want to achieve. It is important before your thought processes are just as important, if not more than how much money, education or status you have when you are trying to achieve the goals that you have set for yourself.

There are some traits that are common to people who have established and developed their mental toughness skills; and these traits include: mental competency, emotional intelligence, resilience, willpower, a winner's mind, the ability to focus, they surround themselves with people who are mentally tough, and they avoid trying too hard to go against the grain. They also possess some common habits, one is by leaving the past behind and learning from it by improving the present situations. There are even some interesting techniques that you can use to let go of the past if it is still weighing on your mind. You can try holding a ceremony to let go of the past and move on positively.

There are a number of reasons that you should develop your mental strength, and one of the primary reasons is so that you can be more productive. Did you realize that people who have a great amount of mental strength get more things done? This is because they are able to concentrate and focus. They handle emotional issues when they arise so that they do not become overrun with emotion. Moreover, they manage their time and money wisely. Feeling in control of your life is another reason to develop mental strength. Feeling that the things that take place around you are out of your control is a feeling of powerlessness that can be remedied.

Furthermore, building your mental toughness will help you transition more smoothly through the changes that occur in your life. Mental toughness is needed for everyday life situations because you never know what is going to occur. Additionally, mental toughness helps a person navigate through tough times more smoothly. Mental toughness helps you prioritize. And there are a number of other reasons that a person should develop mental toughness.

There are certain techniques that you can use to build mental toughness. One such technique is to take a long hard look at yourself and evaluate who you are. Evaluate where you are in your life and your values and belief systems. Identify your strengths and weaknesses so that you can strengthen the areas where you need improvement. It is important not to allow your mental energy to be wasted on either things that are insignificant or things which you have no control over. Meditate and reflect on your day at the end of each day. Do not try to be a perfectionist. To develop mental strength, you also want to practice staying calm in high-pressure situations.

Fear and stress are emotions that you experience that have a direct impact on your mental toughness. If you have not taken steps to develop your mental strength, situations that draw out these two emotions may actually weaken you mentally. However, if you have taken the time to develop your mental strength, you should be more prepared to handle both stress and fear and continue on your way to your accomplishments.

Setting and achieving goals in life is very important and developing mental toughness helps you set these goals and get them accomplished. When setting goals, be sure that the goals are ones that motivate you. Also, be sure that they are written down and displayed in a prominent place. Furthermore, your goals should be SMART goals. Move goals into action plans. Be sure to incorporate your goals into your daily routine.

Lastly, it is very important for you to have emotional intelligence due to the fact that life is often about human interaction and emotion. Gaining emotional intelligence helps you to understand your own emotions as well as those of others so that you can identify where negative emotions are coming from and correct them. It also helps you with communicating with others and emphasizing with other people. You can gain some emotional intelligence by writing down the way you feel throughout and at the end of the day, soliciting the opinions of others, stopping and thinking before some interactions and evaluating these interactions later, observing others, practicing putting yourself in situations where you will use your emotional intelligence skills, and learning to take criticism. It is very important that you develop these emotional intelligence skills because people who lack them often experience negative consequences include: getting into frequent arguments, feeling a lot of negative emotions, overly negative opinions of people and situations, behavioral issues, lower performance, lower level of self-confidence, refusing to listen to the opinion of others, blaming others for their own mistakes, and finds it difficult to develop and maintain close relationships. Thus, taking the time to develop emotional intelligence can make your life much easier and go more smoothly.

Thank you for making it through to the end of *Mental Toughness*, let's hope it was informative and able to provide you with all of the tools you need to achieve your goals whatever they may be.

The next step is to put some of the ways to develop mental toughness and emotional intelligence in action and develop some of the common traits that mentally tough people often possess to help to get you on your way toward having a stronger mind that will serve as the foundation for you setting and achieving your goals.

Finally, if you found this book useful in any way, a review on Amazon is always appreciated!

Made in the USA
Monee, IL
21 December 2022

23359039R00085